Daniel Nour is an Egyptian-Australian journalist and a member of Sweatshop Literacy Movement. His writing has featured in *The New York Times*, *SBS Voices*, *Meanjin Quarterly* and *Eureka Street*. In 2020, he won the New South Wales Premier's Young Journalist of the Year Award. He dabbles in improv comedy.

First published in Australia in 2025 by Affirm Press,
a Simon & Schuster (Australia) Pty Limited company
Bunurong/Boon Wurrung Country
28 Thistlethwaite Street, South Melbourne VIC 3205

Affirm Press is located on the unceded land of the Bunurong/Boon Wurrung peoples of the Kulin Nation. Affirm Press pays respect to their Elders past and present.

New York Amsterdam/Antwerp London Toronto
Sydney/Melbourne New Delhi
Visit our website at www.simonandschuster.com.au

10 9 8 7 6 5 4 3 2 1

A catalogue record for this book is available from the National Library of Australia

9781923046573 (paperback)
9781923419117 (ebook)

Cover design by Josh Durham
Author photograph by Kashif Harrison
Typeset in Garamond Premier Pro by J&M Typesetting
Proudly printed and bound in Australia by the Opus group

The paper in this book is FSC® certified. FSC® promotes environmentally responsible, socially beneficial and economically viable management of the world's forests.

How to Dodge Flying Sandals

and other advice for life

DANIEL NOUR

For my parents: this book may be the only child I give you.

Contents

Author’s Note

You can tell many facts, but not a bit of truth. In that spirit, let me explain from the outset that while this is a memoir of my life, it is not a precise account of people, places and events. I have taken liberties that I hope pay off.

Throughout this book, when English characters couldn’t sufficiently imitate Arabic words, I used Franco-Arabic, a transliteration system mixing English letters and numerals. It has many variations, with no strict rules, and adapts to individual use. The words here generally follow a common Egyptian Franco-Arabic style.

Number	Arabic letter	Example	Meaning
2	ء (silent)	2ol	tell
3	ع (*a* or *e*)	3arabeya	car
3’	غ (*gh*)	lo3’a	language
7	ح (*h*)	7ayah	life

Author's Note

How to Die

Lo, as the sun sets, so too will your day end ... probably from a heart condition, for it runneth in the family.

His face has been yellow and gaunt for months, so it is hard to tell at first that Gidoo is actually dead. The lines of his skin have smoothed out and his mouth is open after his last, almost inaudible breath.

It doesn't take long for Mum to start yelling that we need to get him out of the house.

'He travels thousands of kilometres on a boat from Egypt and you can't stand to have him here for a few more minutes?' Dad screams from Gidoo's room.

Mum shouts back that it's 'unchristian' to have a dead body in the house. She is probably referring to Genesis 23, which says, '... bury my dead out of my sight.'

'Don't just sit there looking like a donkey,' Mum says to me. 'Go bring me two onions.' She is cooking for the meal that will follow tomorrow's funeral.

Rising from Gidoo's bedside, I go get the onions from the garage, then go back to his room to be with him for a while longer before the people from St Mina Funerals, the Coptic Orthodox funeral service, come to take the body away. Next to his electric medical-grade bed, which we bought on Gumtree, the IV is still drip, drip, dripping. A small pond of urine has pooled into his catheter bag. I hold Gidoo's cold hand for around half an hour until two swarthy, heavy-set men barge in, lift him easily out of his bed as though they are carrying a rug, put him on a stretcher and drive him away in their van.

Tant Ansaf, Gidoo's sister and Dad's aunty, walks in right after the men leave. She is stout, with thick legs that burgeon into cankles.

'What happened? Last time I checked, he was doing much better. Now, he is gone!' Her little eyes are narrowed.

We've looked after Gidoo for two years. Teta died first and then Gidoo had a severe stroke three weeks later. The burden of care fell on Fareed, my dad, the eldest son, which really meant that it fell on Mum. Every day Gidoo would spit out the mushy food she fed him and then abuse her, saying, 'She's a mean lady. Heya set w7esha.' In the Egyptian community, abandoning an elder is considered as bad as cutting off your own arm, so the implication that Gidoo died through our neglect is too heinous for Mum or Dad to countenance.

'Khalas, Ansaf,' Mum says. 'There is nothing we can do now.' Mum looks exhausted, wrinkles etched around her mouth. Dad's eyebrows are raised, and his shoulders tense.

Tant Ansaf's phone is ringing. I see that it is a Skype call from Gidoo's other sister in Egypt. 'I knew this would happen. I turn away for a second and the next minute, he's dead!' Ansaf shouts into her Samsung Galaxy, storming out as quickly as she came.

At the same moment, Rita, my older sister, walks in, spitting pumpkin seeds from their shells into a small napkin and nodding briskly towards Ansaf. She is clad in spandex and an oversized jumper, the skin around her eyebrows red and shiny from a fresh plucking. She takes in Gidoo's corpse, all of us standing around him. 'Allah yer7amo,' she grunts, before returning to her room to continue watching *America's Next Top Model*. Tyra Banks shouts down our hallway: 'We were rooting for you!'

~

When Rita and I walk into the church the next morning for the funeral service, a thousand heads turn to the entrance to look at us. A whole row of my dad's elderly cousins, women who are all five-foot-one and dressed entirely in black, including the veils on their heads, turn away and start chattering. 'It's all well and good to show up after he's dead,' I hear one say.

Rita whispers spitefully into my ear, 'Look at these judgey bitches,' before going to sit with her bestie, Stephanie, near the front. Tant Ansaf's rumour of Gidoo dying because we weren't watching him has spread quickly. She holds sway in the community because she works in the church cafeteria, which is like a command centre for gossip. Dad's sister, our nosy Tant Carmen, is sitting next to her, the back of her head shrouded in a black veil.

'Hello, habibi. My love, my dear, my dove. I know what you're feeling, I know how sad this is for you,' says Tant Awatef, the smallest of the women. It's too late to escape before she pulls me down to sit near her at the back. 'Did you eat the kousa I left at your doorstep? Your grandad left something for me with your teta but she forgot. It was cash money in an envelope from the church picnic many years ago.'

Uncle Kareem, Gidoo's nephew and Tant Carmen's husband (as well as her first cousin), walks into the church just now. He doesn't like anyone in the family other than his wife because he thinks we didn't give him his proper share of the sale of Gidoo's mixed-business shop in the 90s. He stands at the back with his arms crossed as my father rises to speak.

Up on the stage behind the podium, Dad tells lies about my grandfather: 'He was always so calm ...' (Gidoo had a notorious temper.) 'He was generous with family, friends, even strangers ...' (Gidoo was very tight with money. Once, someone from World Vision came doorknocking at Christmas and Gidoo handed them two overripe mangoes in a plastic bag.) 'He loved all people; he didn't care at all who they were or where they came from.' (Gidoo hated most ethnic groups, including every other type of Arab. He only respected the Chinese, saying they were 'good workers with their twenty-four-hour shops.') 'He was a man of God.' (Gidoo never went to church and often said that church people were all liars and thieves.)

'Good speech,' says Uncle Kareem from the back. 'Best in the West.' He gives the A-okay sign with his left hand to all present.

Finally, the priest rises to read from the Book of Second Corinthians, giving the sign of the cross to the congregation. 'As the scriptures say, he is out of the body and with Christ,' he begins.

'And I am out of pocket, since your teta forgot to give me that money from the church picnic,' Tant Awatef whispers into my ear.

I gear up for the crucial moment: the carrying of the casket. As I am one of three grandsons, along with Shoukry and Ayman, it's important to Dad that I carry the coffin with maximum visibility. This is also when Tant Awatef chooses to continue her story about the church picnic. 'Nobody knew about the catering I did for your gidoo's mixed-business Christmas party. I remember it all. I cooked kofta, mokorona bechamel with extra meat, molokheya, fried chicken drumsticks and then another kind of chicken with vegetables.'

In slow motion, I see Shoukry and Ayman stand up and lurch towards the aisle. They look like chimpanzees because their arms are too long for their bodies and they have never done a leg day. How did I miss this critical moment in the ceremony? When did the priest finish talking? I should have stood up minutes ago. I won't reach the coffin in time but I try all the same.

'Sorry, excuse me, pardon me,' I say to the ladies in black. These women do not even attempt to get out of my way. They are far too old, fat and sad to move. One of them has fallen astride the church pew and is now crying in this new, lopsided position.

There should be four men at Gidoo's coffin: Shoukry and Ayman, to represent their mother, Carmen; Kareem, his son-in-law and nephew; and me to represent Dad, who can't carry the coffin because of his bad back. By the time I arrive at the casket, a second cousin I don't recognise has taken my place, leaving no space for me. With Dad talking to the hearse driver – I can see him giving directions with his arms – none of the men from our immediate family get to hold the coffin. I trail slowly behind Gidoo, feeling the hot flush of shame rising through my face.

Shit, this is bad, I think to myself. Will everyone think we fell out with Gidoo?

'You are a donkey.' Dad tells me right after the other men load the coffin into the hearse, slapping the back of my neck. 'You're eighteen. Meant to be a man. If Gidoo knew you didn't carry his casket to the car, he would wake up and slap you as well!'

We drive to Rookwood Cemetery straight after the funeral in Bankstown, all our cars following the hearse in a maudlin parade. It takes us a while to find the correct plot. There is a lot of standing around and I can hear some of the old ladies exchanging recipes under their breaths between sobs. Malek, my gidoo's brother, is holding on to a walker and connected to a portable ventilator near the coffin, barely alive.

'Abdel Malek,' the priest finally begins, raising his arms towards the heavens.

Dad gently nudges the black-clad priest, whose wooden cross sits atop a giant belly. He whispers to him that Gidoo's name is Abdel Youssef.

Tant Carmen starts wailing. 'Abdel Youssef! Abdel Youssef!' She shakes her meaty hands into the air around her face then slaps her cheeks repeatedly.

There are funeral prayers and Gidoo's next of kin – Dad, Carmen and Kareem – take a shovel from a bucket with a ribbon on it and throw dirt into the grave. I hear Tant Ansaf say to Tant Awatef, 'They weren't watching him when he died,' and, 'Can you imagine dying without being watched, without being seen?' Awatef shakes her head.

All this sorrow and moaning – Arab funerals make me wish I was dead.

'Sa ansa ana kol a7zani hena, sa ansa ana kol 2lamee hena, fi a7dan Yaso3 el 7abib,' everyone sings, off-key. 'I shall forget all my sorrow here, I shall forget all my pain here, in the embrace of Jesus the Beloved.'

The coffin is gently lowered into the grave. There is a moment of silent reverence and even Carmen, who is always muttering something, falls quiet.

'It's a good deal on the tomb ... two for one.' Uncle Kareem shouts out, puncturing the quiet like a gunshot.

Gidoo's children and an array of extended family all head back to Tant Carmen's house to eat. The spread is richly laid with small bowls of baba ghanoush, baked potatoes with cream, a rice pilaf with chicken, beef and vegetable lasagne, spaghetti bolognese and Mum's bamya in a tomato sauce with more rice.

We have barely sat down to eat when Uncle Kareem says, 'Enough small talk. What about the money, people?' Bits of chicken fly out of his mouth like shrapnel as he waves a drumstick in his hand matter-of-factly. In Arabic, Kareem means 'generous', but this is the opposite of Kareem's personality. Once he tipped the waiter at a Chinese buffet but then took it back when he realised that the staff at Five Star Banquet didn't carry change.

Dad says that everyone should get their fair share of the estate because that is what Gidoo would have wanted.

'How would you know what he wanted? You weren't even watching him in his last hours.' Ansaf spits back. She is standing behind Dad and dollops a huge spoonful of baba ghanoush onto a plate for him.

'How can you say that?' says my mother, who has been silent this whole time.

'Don't you start, Samira.' Ansaf points at Mum, slicing the air with her spoon. 'You're not even blood, so you don't get the same share of the estate.' She purses her lips pointedly, her hand reaching for the table.

One of the last things Gidoo said to me before he lost the ability to speak was that he loved all his children equally but that jealousy made people act in crazy ways. He said that we must all be good to each other because 'we can't take anything with us when we leave this dunya.'

'I loved him most ... He was my dearest brother.' Tant Ansaf finishes, swaying from side to side.

'Ansaf, are you okay?' Mum asks.

'Okay?! It's not okay. Not okay to let a man die!' Ansaf's voice is shaky and she starts to stumble back and forth.

'You should sit down,' Dad tells her.

One of the veins on Tant Ansaf's temple grows thick, bulging outwards from her forehead, which is glistening with sweat. The fat fingers of her right hand clutch at her collarbone. She falls.

'Don't worry, Ansaf, we ... here ... for you,' Dad says, eating the creamy baba ghanoush.

When the ambulance comes for Ansaf, she says to one of the paramedics, 'Please make sure someone is with me always.' She spends three weeks in the hospital and one in intensive care before she has a heart attack. Nobody is watching when she dies.

How to Make Kahk

Better to kiss your mother's worn feet than reject a meal at her table.

Mama is rolling out the petit four dough that she uses to make kahk, tea biscuits baked with heaps of butter and coated with a thick layer of icing sugar.

'Mum, what should I do after I finish big school?' I ask. My voice is high and I'm in my favourite Oscar the Grouch jumper, which I got from Kmart. His head pops out of the bin and he wears its lid as a hat.

'Habibi, you can be anything you want to be.' Mum drops little knobs of Turkish delight deftly into the centre of each small mound of dough, folds the dough back over. She is making them for my fifth birthday.

'What if I want to be a lawyer?'

'Yeah, that would be good.' Mum's voice is light, but the metal instrument she uses for crimping the dough scratches against the floured kitchen bench with a sharp screech.

Rita has tied a big pink bow on our German shepherd Sultan's head and is walking him around the house on a leash, pretending she is Princess Jasmine with her friendly tiger. This morning, she used me as a doll, dressing me up in the pink and puffy tulle of one of her own dresses, with Sultan as the audience.

'Or a doctor?' I ask Mum, getting into the game.

'Doctors make very good money and help to heal the sick.' Mum hits back. She places the raw biscuit on the baking tray, shiny with its thin sheen of butter, and reaches for another handful of dough. I watch her for a few more minutes.

Baba likes to eat the kahk with tea, slurping the shay from the cup with his lower lip extended like a shovel before crunching the powdery white exterior of the biscuit and biting down into the gungy Turkish delight in the centre. But he is at work, so my weekdays father figure is *Sesame Street*'s the Count, who, with his accent and massive Arab-looking nose, is strangely comforting.

'And then marry? Should I marry a girl?' At this, Mum laughs loudly, reaching for a sieve, into which she pours Homebrand icing sugar that she sifts over the now full tray of biscuits. 'What if I don't want to get married but travel everywhere and tell big speeches on a stage in a dress? And I'll have my friends Steve and Jeremy with me and kiss them.'

Mum turns the oven dial up, slips the tray onto the highest rack. 'Habibi, that's enough now. Go watch *Sesame Street*.' She wipes the floury kitchen counter down with a wet Chux. She is no longer smiling.

How to Float

A well-fed fish always outswims a hungry man.

I am seven and have just finished swimming practice at Sutherland Shire Leisure Centre. Mum, a strong swimmer, did laps in the big pool while I scrambled about in the shallow end with my instructor, Cayden, in the after-school learn-to-swim classes recommended by Mrs Hayes, my Year 1 teacher.

There I stand in the shower rooms – brown, nervous at the sight of so much white flesh and very embarrassed. Even at the pool, I wear my fanela, the tank top that Mum insists I don in all weather conditions, hot or cold. Take it off in the heat and you'll suffer laf7et hawa, the 'slap of the wind', when a sudden gust cools your sweat too quickly and you can catch a cold or die. Take it off in the cold and pneumonia will follow. I never think to ask why I need to wear it underwater.

Mum and I are looking for an empty shower stall when I see her: a broad-shouldered Anglo woman, naked, tall and strong, with pale skin that has been scorched an angry red from the steam. At first, she seems relaxed, easy. Then she looks at me and freezes. Her lips purse and her nostrils flare. She looks at Mum. 'He shouldn't be here. He's making me uncomfortable with his staring,' she says.

Her cold voice shrivels my infant manhood. I feel the burning rush of shame rising through my neck and colouring my cheeks. Maybe she's right, I think. Maybe Mama was wrong to bring me into the women's hammam. I hide behind my mother, wishing the drain would open so I could slip quietly down the pipes, out of the women's bathroom and out of sight forever.

'You a crazy woman!' Mum shouts, and she proceeds to aggressively soap me down with the sea cucumber loofah she brought from home, turning on the water to maximum pressure.

After Mum drives us back from the leisure centre in complete quiet, I hear her talking to Mrs Hayes on the phone while I'm eating an egg and basterma sandwich in front of the TV. In the *Simpsons* episode I'm watching on Fox8, a group of brown foreigners flail desperately in the water of a lap pool, while the competent American swimmers power easily down the lanes. They move like Blake Colhoun, the strongest swimmer in our class – he makes freestyle look easy.

'Listen here, how dare she talk nasty about my son?' Mum shouts through the receiver. This is followed by a pause, Mum's breath heaving in her chest, then she adds, 'Don't tell me I overreact!' After all, it was Mrs Hayes who told Mum I 'should really have some extra lessons' because I swim 'quite poorly', which was her way of saying that I flop around like a fish out of water.

'My child deserve better and I can complain to principal,' Mum continues.

I bite into the sandwich, the soft egg and sweet, pillowy white roll providing a perfect contrast to the salty, beefy taste of the basterma. 'I am not misunderstood what she said! She was talking nasty!' Mum yells, her face turning redder as I sink deeper into my soft sofa to watch the Simpsons fly through space and time on their soft sofa, over and beyond shame and far away from scary white ladies.

~

In my dreams that night I'm haunted by images of undressing in the boys change rooms. Blake Colhoun and his friends are all rake thin from constant movement, riding their BMX bikes through the national park on the weekends, and from eating white food such as chicken schnitzel sandwiches with mayonnaise. 'Bitch tits,' they taunt, squeezing my nipples and slapping my butt after our Year 1 swim class. 'How come you're shaped like a girl?' I wake up wet and sticky, and shouting, 'I don't want to take my fanela off!' But it's still dark and all I can hear is Dad snoring in the master bedroom down the corridor.

My tummy squelches in the school bus on the way to the pool that morning. The milky tea and Vegemite on toast Mum made me went down too quickly and I had to run to the loo to poop just before we left the sports oval. Blake and his mates are bragging about who will finish freestyle first. I keep my head down, my stomach turning to water again. At the pool, I'm hit with the bracing smell of chlorine. I try to join the 'Platypus' swimmers line as surreptitiously as possible, but Blake clocks me out of the corner of his eye and nudges his mates. They snigger and one of them says, 'Nice shirt.'

When I emerge from the shallow end, my fanela is sopping wet. I follow the trail of water into the boys change rooms. All around me I see pink and white flesh – legs, tummies, feet – and the scathing eyes and shrew-like faces of Blake Colhoun and his mates, Justin and Kyle. They hit each other's bottoms with towels they have twisted into whip-like cords, they play tip, they run in and out of the showers. Kyle, who grew up in a housing commission, is lingering in the shower stall. At first I think there must be yellow cordial pouring down the drain pipe, but then I follow the stream up to its source and realise, with a jolt of shock, that he is using the shower as a toilet.

Watching all this, my sphincter tightens and I know that if I'm to make it out of this hellscape, I cannot let them see my nipples, the large pink eyes adorning the soft protuberances of my obvious boy-breasts. Nor can I let them see my willy. That would be a death sentence, for theirs look like white snakes while mine is circumcised and looks like a sneaky little lizard. To evade their attention, I change around the corner in the barely concealed section separated from the shower stalls by a wall of brick.

In the bus ride back to school, I feel like I've beaten the system, but my smile drops when Mum removes my school sports shirt to find the fanela beneath still sopping wet. Her eyes widen and her pupils dilate. 'You will catch a cold.'

~

At Sunday school, we receive a lesson about the Egyptians drowning in the Red Sea, while the Israelites make it safely to the other side. Our lot have never been strong swimmers, I think, staring at the picture of the handsome soldiers thrashing in the white foam and their horses neighing frantically at their demise. Moses stands on the other side in a galabeya, with his hands open to the skies like a big shot. It's with thoughts of God's punishment still in my mind that I arrive at Wednesday's session.

'Alright, Platypus level, everyone jump in the water.' Cayden declares with the conviction of a prophet. 'Today we're using the paddleboard,' she continues.

I grasp the edge of the board but struggle to get my bearings, balancing my body against the onslaught of feet and thick calves of all the other students who don't swim well, including Daad Hadara, whose giant glasses make her look like a wet owl. In the foamy confusion, my grip slips and I panic, bobbing underwater and flailing for the pool's edge. I manage to get myself to the edge, then glance over at the end lane to see if Blake is looking, but he is confidently breaststroking in 'Shark' level.

Later, in the change rooms, I have to face my pharaoh.

'Did your parents not have to swim in the desert?' Blake asks.

'My mum grew up in Alexandria,' I respond. 'Near Waterloo.'

'Water poo!' he says back, to a round of laughter.

I manage to dip in and out of the shower, willy and nips on full display. Quickly drying myself, I get back into my sports uniform, still dripping and sudsy in parts, and onto the bus intact. Only my spirit is broken.

~

I get home and Mum greets me at the door, smiling. She has just finished her women's prayer meeting and all the other ladies are in the house sipping tea and laughing. She sees my pudgy frame and small downturned mouth, and her eyes go soft and sad.

Another call to Mrs Hayes that afternoon: 'My son is getting the bullying!'

Mum manages to get me to confess the whole story of Blake's meanness, of the yucky feeling I get facing the shower. With Mrs Hayes' help, she gets an appointment at to the community services precinct of Menai town centre to talk to a child psychologist the next Saturday morning.

Mrs Smith, thin and pale and in her thirties, with a neat bob cut that suits her neat, well-rehearsed answers, welcomes us into her office. She sits straight in her chair. Therapist to my left and mother to my right, I feel trapped and confused.

'Daniel, I think it's really important that whenever you're

bullied, you tell the teacher about it straight away,' Mrs Smith says.

'No, no,' Mum interrupts. 'That won't help.'

'Then what would you like me to do for him?' Mrs Smith asks.

'Show him how to talk back,' Mum says, her eyebrows arched.

Mrs Smith erms and umms, and Mum cuts the meeting short. 'You are a useless woman,' she pronounces to the psychologist before ushering me out.

Holding my mother's hand, I look over at Mrs Smith as we leave. She is leaning forwards in her chair, shoulders tight, and her face is that of a white woman who has just seen her first brown penis in the swimming pool shower.

How to Succeed Academically

Wise study brings little gain; a thug is your true defence on the day of trouble.

Dad's gold Rolex flies down his wrist as he slams hard on the brakes and pushes his huge, hairy brown hand into the horn. 'You bloody silly bugger! You smartie!' he shouts at an Anglo-Australian P-plater with a rat's tail. The teenager sticks his hand out the window and gives us the finger before roaring down Narellan Road.

We are Egyptian Protestants, so while it's okay to say things like 'smartie' or 'little smartie', it is never okay to say 'fucking idiot moron', which I can tell from the bulging vein in his temple is what Dad really wanted to say. He never calls me 'fucking idiot moron'. With me, he uses nice words like 'good man' or 'good bub' and only shouts when I get my times tables wrong or my room is messy or I don't do well in a comprehension test.

Actually, I never see him that much anyway because he wakes up at four every morning to open Mid-City Newsagency, the mixed-business shop he owns on King Street near Town Hall Station. Dad usually gets home after 9pm.

It's a long drive from leafy Menai and now I have a maghas-ache. Seeing Dad upset sometimes gives me maghas, but I'm also worried about today's Tournament of Minds state championships at the University of Western Sydney's Campbelltown campus. I try to focus on the game of Snake I'm playing on Dad's Nokia 6210. The dull, heavy clicks of the buttons and the jarring movements of the pixelated reptile don't distract me from the curdling nausea. I don't want to let Dad down.

Only a few days before, he told my uncles how happy he was with me. 'Howa walad zaki 2wi! W kman byetkalem kwayes 2odam el gomhoor! He's a very clever boy! He's a great public speaker too!' They were all standing around the barbecue drinking Tooheys New. My mum and aunties were inside rolling vine leaves.

All my Coptic Orthodox uncles spoke at once: 'Ah, good boy, yeah', 'Tournament like war', 'Play sport but study harder', 'We tell priest to say a prayer for him', 'Where is shish kebab?'

Nancy, my Year 5 teacher, spots us as we walk into the foyer of the UWS Students' Union. Dad has a big belly but is strong, whereas I am short, weak and pudgy. I wish my father looked like the white preacher dad from *7th Heaven* and that I looked like Jack Scully from *Neighbours*. I think I hear someone laughing at us, but it's just a kookaburra.

'You're late, Mr Nour,' Nancy says to me, with a tight-lipped smile as thin as her waistline. We call Miss Powers by her first name because she told us she wanted to be our friend more than our teacher. Maybe that's why she always picks on me in class whenever she gets the chance, shaking her pale, bony finger at me and staring at the flab of my belly with hungry eyes. She's pretty mean for a friend.

'Ah, we always running on Egyptian time, hey?' Dad nudges Nancy's shoulder, a twinkle in his eye. She smiles at him with her weasel face. He leaves me to her but not before saying, 'Yalla, you do excellent in this competition, bub.' Then he goes outside to take a call on his Nokia. I hear him shouting at an Indian man from Telstra. 'No, that's the wrong amount, Rajesh!'

'Please make sure that your dad puts his phone on silent,' Nancy says. She hands me a sticker with my name on it and walks me towards the seminar room where my team are preparing for the debate. Along the way, she runs into another teacher and stops to talk to her about the awesomeness of multiculturalism. Nancy loves Sutherland Shire, with its clean white houses and even whiter people, always telling us how lucky we are to have the Royal National Park and Cronulla Beach right in our backyard. Everyone is proud of Nancy too, because this year she won a teaching award from the Department of Education.

From our classroom drill sessions with Nancy, I know there are three stages to the competition: an outdoor registration section, brainstorming time in the seminar room and an impromptu speech prepared as a group and presented by one lucky student. 'Collaboration is the key criteria for success in Tournament of Minds,' Nancy has told us for weeks now.

Ben Smith, our fat, freckle-faced team captain, is standing in front of our group, a combination of students from different grades who are sitting cross-legged in a circle on the green carpet. They include Ryan Esfehani, an Iranian Baha'i who is always about to cry, and Lisa Cullens, who is tiny even for an eleven-year-old. Kiera Müller, who is sitting closest to Ben, is the one who's been selected to deliver the speech for our group today, which is a big honour. Nancy says that Kiera is a great collaborator, but actually she's a try-hard who only got chosen because she's cute like a von Trapp child with her blonde hair, blue eyes and straight back from years of ballet training.

On the sheet of butcher's paper, which is blu-tacked to the wall, Ben makes a big Venn diagram and writes 'Chinese', 'Samoan' and 'African' in each of the outer circles. Then in the middle, and with huge capital letters, he writes 'AUSTRALIA'. He invites us to shout out words and phrases relating to these categories.

'Fried rice!' says Ryan.

'Aboriginal people!' shouts Lisa.

'Palestine!' I say.

Ben's smile gets bigger with each word. 'This is so great, guys! We're really on the right track and being sooo collaborative. Yummy!' he says like a big wanker. I know that none of this will make a difference because Kiera has prepared her speech in advance anyway.

Still, I decide that this is as good a time as any to share my prepared notes. I tell Ben that I made a vocabulary list and pull it out of my Billabong backpack. The corners of his mouth are downturned.

I read my list, saying each word loudly and clearly: 'Sikh. Melting pot. Korean hotpot. Chinese beef noodle soup. Thai curry. Thai green curry. Penang curry. Pad thai chicken. Jewish. Jerry Seinfeld. Commonwealth countries. Paralympic Games. Louise Sauvage. Postmodern. Lesbian. Gough Whitlam. Ernie Dingo. Inuit. Canada.'

Ben is staring at me like I'm an idiot. His eyes flit sideways to Kiera. 'What were you saying about Africa being really poor?' he says.

The hour passes and Nancy comes in to say that it's time for us all to head to the auditorium. I stand up and walk towards the door. Ben sprints in front of me and cuts off my path. Nancy exits first, then Kiera, then Ben, then Ryan, Lisa and finally me.

We all sit down in the semicircle-shaped auditorium. I see Dad walking into the hall, his shirt darkened with sweat and his chunky Nokia protruding from his pocket. His ringtone is called 'The Buffoon' and usually brings grocery requests from Mum or payment reminders from Coca-Cola Amatil. Now, the phone sits dormant in his pocket like an Israeli landmine in the Sinai. As he moves his large body through the pews to get to his chair, his phone hits some of the white mums on the backs of their heads. Their mouths stretch into tight smiles but otherwise they're perfectly still.

There is a buzzing in my ears that has nothing to do with the whirr of the air conditioning. We all want to win and Kiera is up first.

'Multiculturalism is a concept that Australia invented to stop racism,' she begins, pausing after this opening line to make prolonged, unnerving eye contact with everyone in the front row. She returns to her text, staring at the cue cards. 'There are many ways that Australia is a multicultural country. Firstly, our food is diverse: on a weekday in the Shire where I live, you can enjoy' – at this point she spreads her hand out theatrically, motioning for her guests to enjoy an invisible banquet – 'Lebanese, Greek, Turkish and modern Australian cuisine, which is a mix of Thai food with more normal foods like steak and broccoli.'

Da-da da dum dum dum.

It starts as a soft echo at first but then grows louder and louder. It's the sound of 'The Buffoon' reverberating through the room.

Dad sits relaxed, smiling inexplicably in his chair. My world is ending.

I stare at him, trying to communicate telepathically. These white ladies already hate me, so what must they think of me and my big, hairy, explosive dad now? The ringing stops, just in time for Kiera to begin her second point – something about the importance of different races all getting along and how the Wik decision solved the problem of Aboriginal land rights forever.

The ringing starts again. It's louder this time and one of the parents, a mousy blonde woman in tights and a cardigan, turns her head and stares at Dad. My legs feel like lead. I will the floor to open up and swallow me like a sinkhole did for one of my uncle's best friends in the Six-Day War.

Kiera tries to continue. 'Racism is bad, but unity is—'

Da-da da dum dum dum, da-da da dum dum dum ...

Now Dad also starts looking around for the culprit, as though he's wondering why this fool isn't turning their phone off. Finally the mousy blonde snaps, twisting her head quickly to the side, the edges of her bob bouncing. 'Turn it off! My goodness!' she hisses at him. She turns back to her friend and they both raise their eyebrows in disbelief.

Iranian Ryan, who has the jumpy manner of a prey animal, starts crying.

'Ryan, we'll lose points if you look sad,' Ben whispers angrily, even redder in the face than usual.

Incredibly, Dad's phone is still ringing. What kind of a person calls a man for this long? My father's chaotic search through the sea of baggy polyester that is his trouser leg lasts for an eternity. He is Aladdin trawling through a cave of trinkets for his precious lamp.

'Allo? Yeah, Fareed Nour speaking!' Dad shouts, rising to his feet and stomping out with all the noise and drama of an M1 Abrams tank. The seminar room door slams behind him.

Ryan, who is crying and hiccupping at the same time, asks me if the man with the phone is my dad.

I say, 'I don't know that guy.'

Suddenly, an ear-splitting screech erupts from the auditorium speakers. Nancy rushes to the microphone, nudging Kiera aside and directing everyone to make for the car park in a calm single-file line. We arrive at the emergency meeting point. Five minutes later, Nancy is nervously chatting with the other teachers while tiny Lisa tells me that her dad also had to evacuate his construction site in Penrith once because a builder started a fire by throwing his cigarette into a rubbish pile.

At last, Nancy comes over to our team and explains that we should all go home and that we'll receive the verdict via email once the other schools present their speeches at a centre in Homebush. Dad is still on his phone near the bottlebrush plants, too angry at Telstra to notice that we have an emergency situation.

Once we're on the road home, beyond the five hundred faded McDonald's signs that dot the Hume Highway, Dad asks me, 'Why did that girl get to speak and not you? Is that girl better than you?'

I cry that night, feelings of shame and failure and horniness all swirling around my hormonally pudgy and pimply eleven-year-old body.

The next morning, I come downstairs to find breakfast – two cheese-and-Vegemite toasties and a cup of milky tea – laid out on the kitchen bench. Mum is washing dishes and Dad is drinking coffee from a giant mug that says 'DAD!' He is usually never home this late in the morning but has taken the day off to drive me to school.

The car ride down Bangor Road is silent. Have I done something to disappoint him? Is he angry about Kiera's speech? Shame, hot and strong, rises in my cheeks. I had disappointed my teacher – why else would she look at me with those cold eyes that told me I didn't belong in her classroom? I had betrayed my father too, ashamed of him and his Arab look.

We park and Dad swishes into the deputy principal's office in his shiny trousers, back straight and belly out. I sit in the hallway, tapping my feet against the carpeted floor. Please, Lord Jesus, don't let him embarrass me again.

Dad's gravelly voice cuts through my sad daydreams. 'I don't bloody care what you say about Nancy. She is a racist woman and she is ignoring my son on purpose.'

The two chubby white ladies who run the school office look at each other nervously and continue working as though nothing is happening.

'That's wrong, you can't ignore some students and let others have a chance!' I hear Dad say. 'She hates my son!' His scream bursts out of the deputy principal's office and down the corridor.

Blake and Jackson, also in Year 5 but sportier than me, run in to get some bandaids. They hear the shouting and throw me cocky glances before running out again. Dad marches out of the office angrily. I have to run to keep up with his big strides, up over the asphalt basketball court and out into the car park.

We go straight to Red Rooster. I ask for two crunchy rolls with roast chicken and extra gravy. The cashier stares at my pudgy body with its flabby rolls of belly fat. When I walk out with the two sandwich bags, Dad sees my sad eyes and chunky frame. He takes me by the hand and says, 'You should never feel embarrassed about who you are, habibi.'

How to Be Bi(lingual)

Language is the mask, fluency the act.

'Mama, are we Arab?'

'No, habibi, we are Coptic.'

I turn to her, removing my eyes from the TV, where *Aladdin* is playing, a movie I have watched at least fifty times, because it is my heritage. Agrabah transports me to a world of vast tiled courtyards, where friendly tigers guard tan princesses and a fit, shirtless street rat swings around town stealing bread rolls. I am about to ask another question when I hear, 'There, there, my dear. We'll set it right,' in a lilting, high-pitched voice, and snap promptly back to the screen.

My eyes widen, taking in the sight of the creamy short jacket and puffy pants of Princess Jasmine's dad, the Sultan, who is prancing across the TV. As a grown man, the Sultan, who is cute and fat like me, with a neat white beard and a turban that bears a massive gemstone, should really know better than to spend all his time playing with toys. But he is sweet and says things like, 'Splendid! Absolutely marvellous!' while never letting his daughter leave the house.

Mum brings me a mortadella sandwich, then a plate of home-fried chips on a paper napkin with a splotch of tomato sauce, then a cup of pulpy, sour orange juice. I'm trying not to think about the speech I have to give tomorrow, which I've carefully written on A4 paper that I have cut out into little squares and paperclipped together. The topic of the speech is 'My heritage'.

The stars are peeking out from the darkened sky outside the living room window by the time I get up for my shower. I can make out two constellations: the Southern Cross, for our Lord Jesus who died to wash away the world's sins; and Orion's Belt, which is aligned with the pyramids of Giza. This is what the British voice said in the World Book '97 video I watched, at any rate.

I traipse barefoot across the cold hallway tiles and into the gleaming imitation-marble bathroom to find that Mum has already laid out a soft white towel and my Aladdin-themed flannel pyjamas, which have a pattern of the monkey Abu choking out the red parrot Iago with his two furry hands clawed into tiny fists. Iago's tongue is curled out of his beak in a ribbon, but you don't feel sorry for him because he's so obnoxious. He reminds me of my classmate Josh Reynolds, who never shuts up and whose head is too big because of some cranial problem he had in childhood. You would feel bad for him about his head, but he complains like a wuss whenever you ask him to play fourth in handball or to shut up during silent reading time.

As the steam of the water beads against the shower pane, I can make out the shape of Tyler Anderson, our Year 6 captain, tan and shirtless through the blur. I remember running into him last week in the line for hot chips at the swimming carnival, and the way he smiled at me and let me go first. Then he asked if I was Egyptian, which my sister, Rita, has been telling me to deny.

'If you tell people you're Egyptian, they'll say you're a terrorist and beat you up.' Rita goes to school in Bankstown, where the cops are always arresting kids for shanking each other with penknives.

That day I forgot to lie and said yes to Tyler, looking down at my stomach and clutching my change in one hand while feeling the sick note I had Mum sign in the other. Rita had written it for me and it said, 'Daniel is unable to participate in the swimming carnival today because he is unwell.' I had used the same line at the athletics carnival earlier in the year.

'That's really cool that you're from Egypt.' Tyler said.

Later, Tyler won the 200-metre freestyle and he smiled at everyone from the podium, the sun shining through his dark, thick hair.

I turn the faucet off and step over the Nefertiti bath mat, facing the mirror where my willy, small and red like Iago, emerges from the steam. It's sitting in its nest of black pubes. My eyes lift up over my body, past my belly and onto my face. It's a cute face, round and dark like an olive, with brown curls like a halo around my head. I look a bit like the cherubic angels on Mum's dresser table, one on each side, slightly lifted on their tiny toes and pudgy ceramic cankles.

Walking back to my room, I pass the living room to see that Mum is eating pumpkin seeds and spitting out the shells into a pile on the pleather sofa and Dad is chewing a bony cut of steak at the bench. That's when I hear Lee Lin Chin, an Asian lady on the TV news, say that America is asking Egypt to hand over the terrorists who flew two planes into the World Trade Centre in New York City. Dad shakes his head and keeps eating, but Mum stops chain-spitting seeds and turns to me. One of the shells dangles limply from her lower lip but doesn't drop.

'We are not Egyptian, we are Coptic. We are from pharaohs. If anyone says what are you, what is your country, say you are Coptic like the pharaohs,' Mum says to me. Then she changes over to the Egyptian satellite channel to watch another episode of *El Hajj Metwalee's Wives*, a series about a man who lives in a big apartment in Cairo with all four of his wives.

In bed that night I see myself as an Ancient Egyptian – sandals, a single black braid on my shaved head, eyes drawn in kohl. My stomach flutters, even though I'm now warm in my Aladdin pyjamas. 'Yeah, I'm Egyptian; that's our culture. We invented language and used the stars to guide the pyramid builders,' I say to Tyler Anderson. He smiles at me and touches my shoulder with his hand, then he brushes my cheek with the back of his palm: cool as my pillowcase.

~

During recess I disappear into the boys toilets to change into Gidoo's old galabeya, which is a bit too long for me but fits right around the thighs, waist and chest, because at twelve years old and barely five feet tall, I'm pushing 55 kilos. It's embroidered with ornate green papyrus reeds and orange flowers, and even though it's made of flowy cotton, it scratches when my legs brush against its cheap fabric.

My Lawrence of Arabia look draws stares as I sit in the pews, waiting for Josh Reynolds to finish his presentation about Stonehenge and why some fugly old Tetris blocks standing in the English countryside are an important part of his heritage.

The tiered audiovisual suite at Bangor Primary School has twenty green carpeted steps that form a semicircle around a central stage area. At the back of the stage sits a giant screen connected to an iMac G4, which is in a tangerine orange and looks like a fishbowl full of batteries.

'Stonehenge was privately owned until 1918, when Cecil Chubb donated it to the British government. It's amazing to think that this impressive monument is even older than the pyramids!' As Josh Reynolds finishes his interminably boring speech, the tips of my fingers tingle with anticipation at my turn to present on my heritage.

'Daniel Nour will now present on Egyptian history,' Mrs Harris says. She is wearing a muu-muu with safari animals on it and her small tummy hangs out beneath her flat little breasts.

I'm not sure how old she is but I imagine it's anywhere between forty and sixty. She's always on a diet and eats a box of salad during her lunch duty.

Lifting my galabeya, I make my way gently down the steps. I pull out the floppy disk from my pocket and poke it into the iMac. It buzzes and whirrs with promise, and up flashes my slideshow with the World Book video of the pyramids. Arabic-sounding crooning – exotic yet predictable – washes over the audience, lulling them into a trance as they enjoy aerial shots of the three pyramids of Giza.

I stare into the pale faces before me, which are all tilted up and cast in yellow light from the sandstorm being broadcast out of the projector. Quietly, I lift a tea towel from the tray of Mum's basbousa at my side, causing the white film of snowy icing sugar on top of the round, golden butter biscuits to puff dramatically.

'Good morning, class,' I say, channelling the same fake politeness I use when forced to talk to Tant Carmen. 'Today, I'll be talking about my heritage.'

The tray is shared around the room: I know Australian people love sweets and are undiscerning about their preparation or varieties. But I can see that some of my classmates' eyes are already glazing over. I feel a jolt of desperation. Something wild courses through me, the tingly excitement telling me to go for it. I hear a swell of music and Genie's voice introducing the fabulous Prince Ali. I straighten up and clear my throat.

'First,' I begin, waving my hands dramatically, 'I'll perform a traditional Coptic blessing.' No one in the room has any idea what a Copt is, so I have free rein. I close my eyes for effect, muttering nonsense syllables that I strung together five minutes earlier.

'Alah … beyaa nafistaa!' I say, drawing out the words as though they carry ancient weight. I wave my arms like a sorcerer, flicking my fingers as if releasing my magical power into the room. The effect is immediate. A few kids lean in, their eyes wide. Perfect.

I have borrowed this tactic from the character of Jafar in *Aladdin*. He is darker than Aladdin, with thicker lips, and I surmise that this means he is more inclined to evil. He is a great showman with his snake-headed staff and plush black-and-red galabeya.

'This,' I say, gesturing to the basbousa with an exaggerated flourish, 'is what the pharaohs ate.'

A few eyebrows shoot up. Bingo.

'Semolina cake,' I continue, with the authority of a history professor, 'was served in silver plates in the castles of the kings. Cleopatra herself probably had a piece right before meeting Julius Caesar and killing herself with snakes.'

'It's yum.' Tyler Anderson says.

'Yep, just like the pharaohs used to have.' I cross my arms, nodding sagely, as if I have personally consulted Ramses II on the recipe. All fifty students eat it up – the cake and the story.

'Anubis, Thoth and Ra Ra Ra!' I incant, clicking play on the next World Book video, which is of King Tutankhamun's tomb, with grainy black-and-white footage of golden head masks and ivory statues.

I read from my prepared notes. 'The pyramids were discovered in the year 1903 by Howard Carter, who was a British man with a great big moustache and an even greater interest in Egyptian history.'

To add some spice, I perform a little zigzag dance, hands out and neck moving side to side, in my best imitation of the dancers from Michael Jackson's 'Remember the Time' video clip.

'King Tut's curse was meant to guard the secrets of the pyramids, and when Howard discovered them, everyone in his expedition died. His wife caught pneumonia, his sister's husband had a stroke on their wedding night because he wasn't that into her and, worst of all, all his Egyptian servants died because they caught the mummy's curse of the tummy, which is like diarrhea but, as there was no Hydralyte back then, they just shrivelled up from inside. So, if you're interested in magic and mystery, go no further than Egyptian history!' I end with a flourish and decide to bow.

Everyone claps politely and Mrs Harris gives me a thumbs up. 'Any questions, class?' she says.

Tyler Anderson throws his hand straight in the air. His school shirt fits him just right; he looks fit and his glasses frame the golden skin on his face nicely.

'Daniel, do you speak Arabic? Can you say something to us in Arabic?'

All eyes turn to me expectantly. Even Mrs Harris looks curious.

I can understand a little Arabic, but really I can't speak much at all. Still, Tyler is looking at me with his nice eyes. The show must go on.

'Yeah, sure. What would you like me to say?' I feel lighthearted, and my fingers and toes are tingling.

'How about you give us a blessing, Daniel?' Mrs Harris wipes her syrupy fingers on her muu-muu. 'Maybe something from your church,' she says, reaching for another slice of basbousa, which is probably a million points on WeightWatchers.

I enter the spirit of the song like Aladdin went into the mouth of that sand cave: '*Habibi ... la la ... shama da nara ... Hubba baba ... la di daa ...*' Then I take a breath and look up, begging the Holy Spirit for the next line. '*Ali Baba ... mashallah ... wahaha ... Rumi ... rumi ... falafel ... tarama ...*' Next I say, '*Salam alaykum ...*' I heard those words once in a mosalsal. I add them, despite the fact that we are not Muslim. I say the following words in quick succession, for they are all great foods: '*Ba2lawa ... hummus ... za'atar.*' Again I end with a flourish, my short arms rising straight up to the heavens. '*Hena jena ... wah wa ... shami ... Shakira ... ya habibi ...*'

A round of applause. Mrs Harris is clapping while shoving food in her mouth, Josh Reynolds is picking his Stonehenge teeth and Tyler is whooping and hollering. I feel huge and tall, like the colossus of Ramses at Abu Simbel – maybe I don't look so bad in my galabeya after all.

People slap me on the back as I walk out of the audiovisual room in my gown. Even Josh Reynolds shuts up as we walk as a group towards the 960 bus stop down Menai Road.

'That was great, Daniel. Really interesting,' Tyler says.

My chest feels huge. 'Oh yeah, thanks, mate. Just my culture, you know.'

'I wish I had an interesting culture. My parents are just from Scotland,' he says back.

I don't know what to say to this so I just nod and stare at Tyler's neck, which is golden and strong, standing proudly out of a collar that is starched hard as cardboard.

We board the bus with a bunch of Year 3s and 4s, who shout and jump up and down, throwing a tennis ball back and forth along the carriage. Tyler sits next to me. His chest is upright and tapers into a thin waist, and he shows off his straight white teeth when he turns his head to laugh over his shoulder. He has a voice that's deeper and louder than mine, which he uses to tell off the younger kids.

The crowd on the bus slowly peters out, becoming emptier and emptier, and because I'm almost the last stop on the line, I have time to think about my speech. The huge bubble of pride I feel melts slowly into a puddle. I feel weird. Like the words weren't honest. Like I lied.

An hour later and I'm planted in front of the telly. I decide to watch *Aladdin* again.

I love Aladdin – he's so fit as well as funny and he sings really beautifully. Jasmine is pretty like always and silly old Sultan is so cute and funny with his grown-up toys. But then there's Jafar. It's like I'm seeing him for the first time.

He walks in, all towering and creepy, with his long black-and-red robe swirling around him. He's got this pointy face and a huge hat with a glowing red jewel on it, and you can tell right away he's up to no good. His gold snake staff is super shiny, and whenever he holds it up, it hypnotises people with its glowing eyes – it's totally freaky. Then Aladdin lies, pretending he's a prince when he's actually poor. He sells out his heritage and culture and it feels really cheap. Maybe he really is just a street rat. Still, his chest is so smooth and his smile is so handsome.

I flick over to ABC Kids. Mum is cutting lettuce leaves in the kitchen and I watch *Silversun*, a space-themed show where a fifteen-year-old guy in tight-fitting spandex captains a space ship. He reminds me of Tyler Anderson.

'Habibi, Mrs Harris says she was impressed with you speaking Arabic today.'

I mute the TV and look at Mum over in the kitchen. Her mouth is kind of tight, like she's trying not to smile but also not sure what to think. There's a twitch by her temple as she chops the lettuce super-fast, and she glances at me while slicing, as if she's waiting to see if I'll mess up.

This will require my best performance yet.

'Oh no, Mum ... that was Coptic.'

How to Offer Hospitality

A fat belly brings derision but is the envy of the skinny man in winter.

Amu Rashid walks in like Our Lord entering Jerusalem on Palm Sunday. His hair is brushed in such a severe side part, so thick on his scalp, that it looks like a wig. With his brown cherubic face, he radiates good health.

'Ya a7la naas, ya hala ya hala: shoof kol el 7abayeb,' he says, like he's never seen people before.

There's a flurry of excitement: it's a big honour when a visiting preacher comes to your house for dinner. Rita, who is in Year 11 and has just started smoking, loves him because he does good impersonations of all the women at church during his sermons, like he's Eddie Murphy from the *Raw* special. Mum and Dad also think he's funny. Only I am nervous, not knowing how to act when he shouts about how to repent or be overcome with the Spirit.

Amu Rashid tousles my hair and goes to sit down with Dad in the special lounge room, which we call the Duke of Windsor suite because it's reserved for royalty. There are paintings of Egyptian tombs in frames on the wall, and if you look closely next to the pharaohs being led into the afterlife, one of the pictures shows the foreleg of a calf being cut off while the animal is still alive; its mother is in distress.

Now Amu Rashid stands to pray. I can feel the movement of the Spirit, or maybe that's just gas. My mind drifts to all the food Mum has made, the smell of overcooked canola oil powerful like the petrol fumes that woo me to bliss at our local Caltex. He says a prayer of blessing, asking God to grace us one by one.

'Ya Rab, barek hazie el beit, barek 3amo Nour w Abu Nour w Rita w Nour, b esm el Masee7.'

'Ameen. Ameen.' A resounding chorus of thanks.

Mrs Fowler, my history teacher, told me about how the Hebrew word Amen was translated into 16th-century English when Bibles were being mass-produced because of the Gutenberg press. I wonder why it didn't get changed to 'Say that!' or 'I agree, mate' or 'I know dat's right!' which I sometimes hear on *The Fresh Prince of Bel-Air*.

'Ya akh Rashid, we haven't made anything special, just light, simple food.' Mum smiles and dabs at her brow with a serviette. Though the smile shows her teeth, her eyes are frozen. It is a fake smile. Mum has been cooking all day, chopping, stuffing and frying. Dad too has spent his Sunday afternoon, his last chance to recover before another big week at the mixed business, vacuuming the entire house and grunting about how filthy we all are. I just want some time alone to study for my Year 8 history exam tomorrow on the topic of Ancient Egyptian religion, but instead we have to roll out the red carpet, and Rita and I have to play along.

Mum lifts a thin tablecloth that has doily-style embroidery on it. There is mokorona bechamel (a traybake of penne swathed in a cream sauce, interlaced with minced beef), ta3mia (Egyptian falafel), la7ma b el batates (bony steaks of beef and potato baked on the stove in a tomato sauce in one of my mum's big red Bessemer pots) and my favourite of all, ferakh panne (chicken cutlets coated in breadcrumbs and fried in oil until golden and crispy). There's also a plump chicken, stuffed with freekeh and fragrant with seven-spice powder.

'Ah, Samira, you know I shouldn't be eating this kind of food because I have sokkar now. But just for your sake, I will try some of everything.' Amu Rashid uses the word 'sokkar' instead of 'diabetes' because in Arabic we say, 'I have the sugars.'

My stomach is making squelching noises. Beneath my pink tracksuit pants that used to belong to Rita and my comfy Lowes jumper is my soft, tender body and thick fourteen-year-old thighs. I want to dip the chicken cutlets into the MasterFoods tomato sauce with my bare hands. I want to gobble up the mokorona bechamel, the creamy richness of it coating my tongue. I want to tear into the chicken, the greasy animal fat leaving a slick film around my lips. All I want to do is eat, but it's rude to start before the guest of honour.

'Tell us how you lost all the weight, Amu Rashid,' Rita asks, looking like she's settling in for some good entertainment.

'I cut mokorona, I cut rice, I cut bread ... Wallahi, Rita, I eat half as much as I used to.'

Seeing Amu Rashid in the hard outline of his polyester jacket, padded in the shoulder, reminds me of *Terminator 2: Judgement Day*, which I watched last week in Rita's bedroom while our parents were having a prayer meeting downstairs. What is beneath his waistband, I wonder? If he were to cut his arm with the chicken knife Mum has put next to the plump bird she bought and stuffed, would it reveal an unfeeling, steel animatronic arm like Arnold Schwarzenegger had when he scared those Black people and told them to 'listen to me very carefully'?

'Just a little for me,' I say, offering my plate to Mum.

'You are on a diet now?' Amu Rashid laughs and Mum, Dad and Rita join in cheerfully.

Rita slaps the table. 'This guy's hilarious,' she yelps.

But as Amu Rashid plunges the chicken knife into the bird, which is a big honour, I feel it is my soft flesh that he is stabbing. He is carving me open, laying bare my insides with his incisive comment about my weight. Mum's eyes are on me and I look down and away.

'Tell me, ya Fareed, what is happening these days in this society?' Amu Rashid asks Dad.

'Ah, ya Rashid, what can I say? Sin, sin has flourished across all homes.' Dad is excited to be singled out for expert opinion, like he's Brian Henderson commenting on the Wik decision. 'Here, a man can marry his own dog.'

'Ya.' Amu Rashid says the Arabic expression for 'wow', and cuts into a piece of chicken. 'That bad, aye?'

It reminds me of the story Amu Rashid told us last week, about two young men who had fallen into the 'great sin' together in Egypt. 'They were like brothers; they were good friends. Sin has spread, my friends, sin has spread. He did it with him, the university student with his younger friend. He came to me crying.' I looked up from the pew where I was half-asleep – this was like nothing I had ever heard.

Amu Rashid now turns his attention to me, his eyes glinting under the light of our chandelier, shimmering with its many faux-crystal baubles.

'Do you have any little girlfriends at school, ya Danny?' Amu Rashid asks.

Dad slaps my shoulder with his giant hand. 'Ah, he's a bit young for that.'

'Not too young. I have Shawky, Mina and Albert, and they all have little girlfriends.' At this, Amu Rashid unfurls his wallet to reveal photos of his three sons. They remind me of troll dolls with their insane smiling faces, stout bodies and kinky, unkempt hair. 'I make sure they play soccer and even lift weights at the weekend. Boys these days look like girls: they sit all day in front of the TV, they don't exercise, weak!' Amu Rashid says.

Dad nods at this and Rita adds, 'That's for damn sure,' fondling the packet of Marlboro Reds she is hiding in her tracksuit pocket. My face feels hot. Mum turns to look at me with an encouraging smile. I remember a cartouche of Isis covering Osiris with her feathers.

'Ah, a beautiful meal, ya okht Samira,' Amu Rashid finally tells Mum, patting his belly. The belt holding up his polyester trousers must have come undone at some point during the meal and the buckle hangs open limply.

'La2a, la2a, you have to save room for dessert,' Mum advises with tired eyes and another stiff smile. As we all move back to the Duke of Windsor suite, Amu Rashid stretches out his hands to declare a sudden blessing.

'Ya Rab. Bless this house. Let it be a thoroughfare of mercy to all who come here. Let it be a source of light and of blessing. Fareed, Samira, Rita, Daniel. Ameen. Ameen.'

The same mouth that blesses also curses, I think to myself plaintively, holding in a fart.

While everyone is eating basbousa and drinking tea, I take my plate upstairs, sit at my desk with its small lamp and open my textbook to a post-it note that marks the 'Hymn to the Nile': 'Hail to thee, O Nile. Who manifests thyself over this land, and comes to give life to Egypt … Watering the orchards created by Re, to cause all the cattle to live, you give the earth to drink, O inexhaustible one!' I doodle pictures of the Eye of Horus for an hour, exam nerves tingling in my belly as I read about Egyptian burial practices.

That's when I hear Amu Rashid lumbering up the steps. Whenever a visiting Man of God is in our city, Mum and Dad give him the fold-out guest bed in the upstairs lounge that sits between my bedroom and Rita's, which means we have to pass a grunting priest or a snoring deacon whenever we need to use the bathroom.

I feel frustrated, and a strong urge rises from my belly, a different kind of hunger. I rapidly type 'Ancient Egyptian, naked' into Google and slam the Enter key down, hard. Dwayne 'The Rock' Johnson appears before me, naked except for a loincloth and tanned a dark brown to play the role of the Scorpion King in *The Mummy Returns*. Looking at the image, my thighs feel itchy, my face feels hot.

That's when Mum comes in. She sees the picture of the scantily clad man. I stare at her. She stares at The Rock. We stare at each other in silence. After a moment that takes four millennia, she asks if I'm ready for my exam and I say, 'I'm not ready yet, but when I am, you'll know.'

She kisses me once on the cheek and her eyes are sad. 'Don't mind Rashid, he is just a silly man.' She gently closes the door.

As I lay down to bed, horny and overfull, I hear Amu Rashid through the thin wall. He's calling his three troll kids. The sound of the Skype call reverberates loudly down the corridor – he must be using the shared computer in the hallway. I hope he doesn't find the history tab, where I looked up 'Greco-Roman wrestling naked' after learning about the Olympics in Mrs Fowler's class last week.

'Habaybee! Wa7shtoni! I've missed you all. Yes, I bought the

Oreo cookies. And the PlayStation game, yes. No, I'll be back soon. Yes, I'll be back!'

I fall asleep dreaming of a shirtless Arnold Schwarzenegger. He is returning on the clouds, wielding a crucifix rifle that shoots thorns. Each shot cracks the sky with a holy *snap*. His eyes glow with judgment; the clouds part. He yells, 'Amen, amen, amen!'

How to Direct the Dramatic Arts

A clear voice in the closet is worth more than a muffled one on the stage.

'Trent, habibi, all I'm trying to say is that my dad won't like it if you kiss me in the living room. We have to wait until we're alone.'

My script is going right to plan. Rita is doing a great job in the role of 'Marina – Egyptian fiancée' in the play I have written about a pair of star-crossed lovers separated by Aussie and Egyptian heritage and differing views on sex before marriage. There's a lot of pressure, after all, to deliver a stellar play for the last night of our annual Bayside Gospel Chapel youth conference, which is taking place over my Year 9 Christmas holidays.

The audience sit in raked pews in the auditorium of the Collaroy conference centre. The whirring air conditioner makes the space cold and dry.

'Honey, why do you have to be so uptight? Why can't you be more like Aussie girls? Just take it easy, mate.'

At this, a round of laughter from the audience, which includes my dad and Tant Carmen. Bassem, who is playing the role of Trent in this family rom-com, is the show pony of our youth group. With his fair skin, he is the nearest thing to an actual white person in our community.

'Trent, what will my parents say about you not being Egyptian?' Rita begins.

'Well, I don't know, Marina, but I love you, babe, and isn't true love all that matters?' Bassem answers, in an exaggerated *Home and Away* drawl.

'True love? That doesn't count for anything, idiot. They won't accept you unless you work as a doctor or a pharmacist – and you're a bloody tradie!' Marina snaps back.

I'm beginning to relax now that the actors have found their rhythm, but earlier today, I was a hot mess.

~

Father Constantinos walked around the sleeping cabins, waking everyone up with a bell. Nobody had slept well. My cousins Shoukry and Ayman had spent all night running in and out of the girls' rooms, and their noise had kept me awake so I was feeling wired and edgy. Strange new feelings often kept me up now that I was fifteen.

I hurriedly dressed, wearing my collared blue-chequered Jay

Jays shirt, knock-off Adidas sneakers that my uncle bought me from Shubra and stretchy-fit Kmart jeans, and ran out into the cool morning. The smell of sweat was still strong in my nose and the image of Bassem's hairy, muscular leg hanging off the bunk bed still clear in my mind.

Walking through the throng to the conference centre, I saw Bassem and Rita kissing on a bench under a tree. A wave of righteous indignation crested in my chest. 'Wow, guys. This is so not pleasing to the Lord!' I shouted.

Rita cast her eyes down, suddenly becoming very interested in a twig. Bassem stood up, hands out and chest puffed. 'Bro, why are you so uptight?' he shouted back.

I ignored him and continued walking huffily to the auditorium. When I arrived, it was to hear Father Constantinos singing the hymn 'Again the Morn of Gladness', but to be honest, it felt more like the Morn of Sadness.

It was weird but I felt kind of angry at Rita. Why did she always have to take up so much time with Bassem? There were definitely things I wanted to talk to him about, like the new Lord of the Rings: The Return of the King game on Xbox where you could play as Gandalf, even brandishing his sick staff. I also wanted to make him listen to 'What You Waiting For?', the new Gwen Stefani song, on my MP3 player. We could share headphones! I'd be heaps okay with that.

Bassem walked in, late as always and smelling of Lynx Africa, the fragrance sweet but woody. He stood in front of me with his strong shoulder blades flaring beneath his football shirt.

We all had to wear deodorant now, since Father Constantinos reminded us that fifteen-year-olds stink.

At breakfast, I sat in the cafeteria at the end of the table, with Bassem showing Shoukry and Ayman a grainy photo of girls from Our Lady of the Holy Cross church, which he had taken from their Year 9 group photo with his Sanyo flip phone. They all shared a deep ribald laugh.

'They make them different there, bro,' Shoukry said. I wanted to chime in but didn't think they would care much for what I had to say about *The Two Towers* being the best film of the trilogy and couldn't really think clearly because I really liked Bassem's smell right then – a mixture of cologne and sweat.

Just as Bassem was answering 'Sank za Lord for zat', in a coarse imitation of Father Constantinos, Rita, who had missed morning prayer completely, plonked down next to him.

'Had to do my makeup and you gronks wouldn't let me get my sleep,' she said.

Rita had been experimenting a lot with foundation and blusher lately. Even on the weekends, all she ever did was straighten her hair with Mum's tourmaline ceramic straightener or apply bronzer on her cheeks, so we didn't really talk much anymore. I plunged my knife into one of the poached eggs, but it had the consistency of silicone and the yolk crumbled like the rubble of Sodom.

'You boys playing soccer this afternoon?' Rita asked, her voice high and singsongy, which was never how she talked to me.

'You'd like that, aye,' Bassem answered back playfully, shoving her gently with his shoulder.

'Bro, she'll slow us down,' Shoukry shouted through a mouthful of egg.

I had never really liked soccer much, ever since Dad forced me to play for the Bayside Hawks in Year 1. I would often run the wrong way down the field, and the only trophy I received was 'Most improved' – never 'Man of the match'.

Still, I liked watching the World Cup with Dad. Balls being kicked back and forth. Veins throbbing. Temples shining with sweat. Powerful but lithe men running like greyhounds. Dad shouting at the television, abusing the referee. 'That's a bloody red card, you silly bugger!' he would yell into empty space.

In my reverie, I followed the boys to the field. As Shoukry went to line up and take the first kick, Bassem ran to sit next to me on the sidelines. 'Bro, how come you never play? Don't you like sports? It'll help you lose weight,' he said breathily, still puffing from the warm-up.

'Yeah, I know, but I prefer to watch. You play so good! I'd probably just get in the way.'

'Suit yourself, man,' he said, springing to action and yelling, 'Offside, offside!'

Bassem and I used to talk more, but he had been hanging out with the older boys ever since he started going to a different high school from me, leaving the Shire for Holy Cross High School in Bankstown. I wished he would sit a bit longer with me here on the sidelines rather than play stupid soccer.

I couldn't get my mind off the play tonight. Would Rita, who was sitting next to me filing her nails, be on time or late like always? Had we planned the movements in the scene well enough for everyone to know how to shift the whiteboard smoothly and professionally and not to show their backs to the audience?

I went back to the cabin to shower before rehearsal. The corridor leading to the dormitories was completely silent. If they weren't playing soccer, everyone was at the beach. I undressed to my singlet and my Best&Less undies. I saw a pair of Bassem's boxer briefs stashed in the corner, next to his jeans, which he must have hastily taken off when he was changing into his soccer shorts.

An urgent feeling came over me. Something that would not be pleasing to the Lord was coming – it always did when I felt this way. I went to Bassem's underwear and picked it up. I looked at the stain where urine had touched the fabric in the crotch. I held it to my face. I inhaled deeply. It smelled mossy, sweet but also sour. I could feel blood rushing to my legs. My penis swelled. I wanted to take it to the ensuite bathroom we were all sharing and rub my dick against it. But I heard voices in the hallway and panicked, quickly throwing it back to the ground.

'I am not myself. This is not me,' I told myself. Father Constantinos always told us to remember that there is a fight between the flesh and the new man. The new man must win.

Breathing slower now, I reminded myself that we had to go

back to the stage and perform our parts. I shuffled quickly back up the bush path, letting the room door slam behind me.

~

The audience erupts into a fresh peal of laughter. They love this ethnic humour. I hope they quiet down so that the next few zingers I've written land clearly enough.

Bassem as 'Trent' is now sitting alongside his prospective father-in-law on a couch we have set up for the occasion. Cousin Shoukry is doing a good job of playing an Egyptian father, but then again, he only has a few lines and is mainly expected to grunt.

'Oh yeah, I love Ronaldinho, Amu,' Bassem says.

'He's a good player but he's a faffy boy, always dancing around the field: look at me, look at me, I'm so pretty,' Shoukry says as Marina's Arab dad.

A smattering of laughter from the audience; my shoulders release.

'Now, Trent, tell me, what's your plan with my daughter?' Shoukry asks.

'Well, Mr Amo, Marina is a beautiful girl and ...'

Shoukry suddenly stands to attention: 'GOAAAALLLL! That's a good shot – you're a quick one!'

More laughter. I hear Tant Carmen say, 'My husband is exactly like that.'

'Trent, you seem like a nice young man. But I have to ask,

do you have any experience with our culture?' Shoukry says seriously to his son-in-law-to-be.

'Your culture?'

'Yes, habibi. Egyptian culture. Our food, our traditions, our way of life,' Shoukry answers forcefully.

'Well, I've tried Egyptian food before. It's delicious.'

'Not just the koshari and molokheya, ya 7omar!'

'Ya 7omar' is a cheap shot but my suspicion that it would get laughs is confirmed. People are yelping and snorting. Tant Carmen is slapping her knee, sounding a lot like a donkey herself.

'One tradition we have is no touchy-touchy before marriage. Do you understand about this?' Shoukry continues.

'Mr Amo, Marina is a big girl and can make up her own mind.'

'Mind? She has no mind! She is a good girl and you mind yourself because I mind!'

The final scene, a wedding ceremony between Trent and Marina, has Shoukry playing the role of Father Constantinos, officiating their wedding.

'Do you, Trent, take Marina to be your lawful wedded wifey to the exclusion of all others and no hanky-panky before tonight?'

'Um, I guess so ...'

'And do you, Marina, pretend to agree with all his opinions, cook him nice meal every day and give him five kids?'

'Um ... I'll try.'

'And that's a try from the line!' Shoukry says to wild laughter.

The audience guffaw like jackals and hyenas, and Bassem and Rita hug because kissing would be too risqué. Shoukry proceeds to read Psalm 23, which is this year's main topic for camp, and everyone in the audience joins in.

Then Shoukry calls me to the stage. 'We have to give special thanks to Danny. He wrote this play from his heart. Even though he's a bit dramatic, we love him very much.'

More applause.

'I wrote this to make you all laugh and I hope it's pleasing to the Lord,' I say back, my face hot as hell. Out of the corner of my eye I see Bassem, who is still in his soccer shorts. I'm relieved. He's smiling. And I'm smiling. Because he's smiling.

How to Tell a Story

My child, acclaim may broaden your chest, but it will not warm your soul.

It is a Saturday morning in our light-filled living room and Mum is already deep into her cooking. The sweet, slightly savoury smell of frying canola oil wafts towards me, strong as a drug. It's hard for her to sign my permission slip with her hands sticky from batter and her grey Nokia 2600 wedged between her neck and shoulder as she chats with her sister in Cairo.

My stomach flutters with apprehension thinking about Monday's work experience at 2SSR FM: Sound of the Shire, our local community radio station. Year 10 at Caringbah High is when we have to complete our mandatory work-experience placements. I grab the slip for the three-day internship back from Mum's hand, examining her name, which she has signed in a childlike scrawl.

Mum is just finishing with the last bouftek. She makes each

one the same way. She dips the pink meat into a plate of raw egg mixture, then into another plate of salted breadcrumbs, fragrant with oregano. With her hand covered in gunky batter, she then gently lowers the veal into acrid oil, letting it bubble and fry for a few minutes. It emerges thick, meaty and crispy – tender meat ensconced in a golden breaded carapace.

I'm sprawled out on the couch and Mum walks over mid-call to drop a hot bouftek onto my plate, which is still greasy from my breakfast of scrambled eggs on a sesame-seed bun. She yells at her sister Huda to stop ignoring the Western Union money transfers that she makes from the post office on Saturdays. Through the phone speaker, I can hear Huda say that she doesn't need the cash, which is a polite lie because her daughter is getting married and we all know they don't have enough money to furnish the new apartment. This is called a dowry, which Mrs Dickson says is what Elizabeth Bennet didn't have in *Pride and Prejudice* and is why she had to marry up.

I've been glued to Lord of the Rings on Xbox all morning and I'm about to thrash an orc with Gandalf's staff, but I pause to enjoy the meal. Biting into the meat, I glance at the Tutankhamun clock above the TV – it's noon. I switch on *SBS World News* for my weekend dose of global affairs. My fixation started when I was small, reading *Time* magazine along with *The Simpsons* comics in the back room of Dad's mixed-business shop. That was when I realised 'Africa' was not a single country you could donate to via World Vision commercials. Now, I was a fully-fledged news junkie.

The smell of the veal wafting from my plate mingles with the refined symphonic strings of the news introduction, beginning with violins and brass before crescendoing into a rousing drum solo. The strangely intercontinental voice of Anton Enus, who some of the guys at school call 'Hands-on Penis', floats over the music.

'Good evening. In the Middle East, tensions remain high as Egypt pushes for a ceasefire in the escalating conflict in the Sinai, with regional leaders calling for urgent negotiations. Meanwhile, Australia's east coast braces for wild weather, with heavy rain and strong winds expected to hit later this week. And in entertainment, Eurovision 2005 is just around the corner, promising all the glitz, glamour and outrageous performances we've come to love. With sequins, pyrotechnics and over-the-top acts set to steal the stage, Eurovision fever is sweeping across Australia. Stay tuned for these stories and more on *SBS World News*.'

I feel like a man of the world, and, buoyed by the inspiring whiteness of Anton's stiffly erect collar, I set aside the bouftek to play one of my favourite fantasy sequences: journalist at a press conference in the Giza Sofitel.

'Oh, yes, the crisis in the Sinai is very troubling, but how have you contributed to the deteriorating economy of your own country, Mr Mubarak?' I ask the Egyptian president in perfect Arabic, in a tuxedo with my little handheld recorder. I'm thin and muscular too – no more soft paunch or chunky thighs.

Afterwards, all the press go to a fancy soiree. I walk through the crowd in my sharp tux and eat the finger foods floating on the platters around me while talking to my editor on my own Nokia 2600, which is even nicer than Mum's and has one of those sick antennas that you pull up from the side. Did I mention the food? Really posh stuff: probably chicken sliders or bits of sushi with fried chicken like the ones at the smaller, good food court at Town Hall Station.

Another SBS drum solo rouses my attention. Anton has crossed over to Lee Lin Chin's asymmetric haircut. In an unexpectedly British accent she says that a review of security and counterterrorism legislation is underway. I run into our home office, which Dad has decked out with encyclopedia collections and all the old *Sesame Street* illustrated dictionaries that my sister and I refuse to throw away. Hatching out a plan, I hastily scrawl in the pages of my foolscap notebook, my fingers slipping on the Bic pen due to the bouftek grease. I am writing questions for an 'Arab-Australian community investigation'. My heart swells with pride as I think about writing the exposé to end all investigative journalism, talking to everyday Aussies about their fear of Arabs since 9/11.

'Do you know any Muslims?' I imagine myself asking local white mums. 'Should we build a mosque in Sutherland?' I would put to the Lord Mayor, waving a microphone in his face like the reporters on *A Current Affair*. This last one seems a bit of a stretch but still a good angle, I reckon. I am determined to find out and deliver these powerful, must-hear stories to the public.

Imagining that Anton would do his research, I look up 'racism' in the *Macquarie School Dictionary*, where I have previously looked up the words 'penis', 'homosexual' and 'pervert', which was much more interesting than the adjacent 'prefect'. Next to the word racism, it says, 'the belief that one's race is superior and has the right to dominate others'.

I wipe my greasy bouftek hands on my pants and, just for kicks, pick up one of the old *Sesame Street* cartoon dictionaries, which sit alongside a hardback edition of Chaucer's *The Canterbury Tales* and all of Shakespeare's plays in seven parts. On the front cover, Oscar the Grouch has been defaced with a Bic pen and someone has Sharpied devil ears and a moustache onto Big Bird.

~

I usually wake for school at 8.30am on Mondays: it's just enough time to catch the 960 down Menai Road to Sutherland Station and then get on the train to Caringbah. When I miss the bus, which happens a lot, Mum just drives me to school, complaining the whole way. Today I have to rise at the ungodly hour of seven because I need to catch an additional bus and get off in the godforsaken suburb of Gymea, which is as Anglo as *Home and Away* but too far from the beach to have any of the charm.

When I finally make it to Gymea TAFE at 9.10am, late for my first day of work experience and in the floppy collared shirt I also wear to church on Sundays, I feel a nervous tickle in my belly.

Here comes Leanne, a seventy-something-year-old with a man's haircut like Maria from *The Sound of Music*, wearing a woven cardigan bearing an assortment of badges, including one that says 'Sound of the Shire' and another that says 'No nuclear in Lucas Heights'.

'Oh yes, hi, yes, hi Daniel – bit late, yep, here's the cafeteria, big job Mondays, few shows going on – *Bryan's Backyard Remedies*, *Larry's Afternoon Classics*, happy hour, yes,' she says in a pitchy and breathless gasp.

We walk through the cafeteria and into the demountable that houses the entirety of the 2SSR FM operation.

'You'll be voicing ad placements – Flower Power's a sponsor, council gets a spot too, yes, good, right – do you have the form?'

I hand it over quickly.

'Yes, good good. Well, Bryan will give you the tour. I've got to present the recipes for *Shire Kitchen Hour*.'

Bryan is a seventy-plus, gruff-looking man in an akubra hat and denim shorts leading into thin, pale legs. He stands up from an extremely messy desk and roughly shakes my hand. He reminds me of a parsnip: broad on top, skinny at the bottom and a bit dirty. Also, he smells like cigarettes.

'Now, Daniel, it's really important that we fill out this ad placement form,' Bryan says in a hoarse, rough voice, sliding a slip of A4 paper that has been unevenly cut with a guillotine across the foyer desk. Some sections are already filled in – my name at the top, the show name and the ad length. I scan the form, noting the blank spaces for the advertiser's details and budget. 'Just add in the target audience and frequency, and we'll be all set, set, settt ... *hekh* ... *ekh* ... *ekh*!' He descends into a round of hacking coughs and points to a big folio that says 'ADVERTISING CONTRACTS' as he spits into a tissue.

Out of the corner of my eye, I spot the recording booth, where the 'Recording in Progress' sign has just turned red. Leanne is inside. As Bryan drones on about invoice receipts, my eyes drift over the booth's sleek design.

It has a big stand microphone that pivots on a hinge. There's a wide mixer with knobs to change the sound, and everything connects to a box for recording on the computer. The headphones look like expensive noise-cancelling Bose ones and the speakers play back the music to the host. A huge multi-tiered CD stacker sits at the edge of the circular desk, which wraps snugly around the presenter. Finally, the soft panels on the walls make the sound better. I will put my work experience here in my résumé and then land a job at the SBS. The image of myself at a press conference materialises once more in my mind's eye.

I turn suddenly to Bryan, cutting him off mid-sentence. 'When do I get to record my ads?' I ask.

'Ah, mate, all in good time.'

'Can we do it right now?'

'Ah, you're a cheeky one. Usually I'd say no, but I can see you have that fire in your belly, so let me see what I can do. In the meantime, work on these forms.' And with this, Bryan adjusts his akubra and goes outside, where I can see him out of the side window of the demountable smoking three Winfield Blues in quick succession.

Leanne ends her segment with, 'So that's how you make peanut butter brittle. Join us next week for a series of special crumbles', and emerges red-faced from the booth. She says something about a hair appointment, which seems like a waste because I could honestly replicate her look with an iron and a table. She leaves for the day.

A full afternoon of filing passes. Bryan comes to check on me occasionally and tells me to go for lunch at the dull Gymea TAFE cafeteria, a big room with three sets of tables and chairs and a butch woman in a netted bun behind a counter. I order a chicken roll, which is claggy with too much mayonnaise, and a desiccated chocolate brownie wrapped in several layers of cling film.

Back at my desk, I hear the announcement segment for *Larry's Afternoon Classics*. I didn't even notice him coming in. Larry dresses completely in shades of brown: khaki pants, beige shirt, greige cardigan. He has a lumpy, long physique and a head like a potato that Bryan might pluck fresh from the earth. His voice is low, deep and surprisingly smooth.

'Welcome to *Afternoon Classics*, where we ask the question: what is a classic?' Larry begins. 'Simon and Garfunkel have classic qualities, but are they really the masters of their craft?' At this, Bryan rolls his eyes and goes outside to smoke some more. 'Some say that the Greeks first defined the classical form when their choruses of music wafted up the high walls of the

Parthenon. What of Beethoven? Yes, he too was a classicist.'

I've also heard the Greeks invented sex toys, I think. I go home deflated and retreat into Middle Earth, where I slay orcs until I fall asleep.

By the next morning, I've graduated to the front desk because Bryan is sick – probably with emphysema. In a high-pitched, eager voice, the kind I think they would use at the expensive perfume counter at Myer, I say, 'Welcome to 2SSR FM: Sound of the Shire, how can I help you today?'

Along with calls from India about whether we would like to upgrade our internet provider and whether we feel we are getting good value from our electricity provider, every now and again an actual listener will call in. One woman tells me off for twenty minutes: we shouldn't host the local mayor's weekly report because he's a left-wing communist who supports too many migrants in our local community and is terrible for businesses including her daughter's hairdresser.

Another man, who talks in a whisper, tells me the history of the radio station and how he served in Crete and Gaza in World War II, then says that they always have 2SSR FM playing in his nursing home in Kirrawee. I feel sad for him, but then, remembering that I'm on the job, I straighten up and say, 'Thank you for your comments, sir. I'll pass them on to station management,' and make a little note in the callers logbook I'm supposed to fill in.

For lunch, I have a cafeteria tuna roll, which is more roll than tuna and more sawdust than roll, and a very sweet hot chocolate from the vending machine. Mum made me bamya and rice, but I feel more like an employee eating the cafeteria rations.

At my desk, I remember how Father Constantinos once told us that God helps those who help themselves, so I write out my own version of the mayor's council announcement. It's a little more upbeat and uses the active voice: not 'Council has said ...' but 'Council says ...'; not 'Should you like to contact council ...' but 'Contact council today!'

I walk over to Leanne, who is putting loose staples into a tiny box with an expression of intense focus: eyes squinty, hair flat.

'Hi, Leanne, I know I was only supposed to do this at the end of the week, but I'd love to record my own advertisement today ... Actually, here's a new script, something pretty simple.' Handing over the script, I feel my insides doing somersaults.

'Oh yes, short, need to mention Mayor's visiting hours, yes yes.' She scratches through a few lines with a felt-tip pen that has been worn down to the nub. 'Good, record it before Classics, haircut this afternoon,' and with this she exits for, I guess, another haircut.

The booth lies open before me, a glimmering portal leading to a world of glamour and UN press conferences where I say things like, 'Daniel Nour, *SBS World News*,' or 'Minister, our investigation reveals mass corruption.'

I sit down to record my audio. I've received no training, so I fiddle with the dials and hit a button that says record.

'Attention, listeners. Your local council is committed to providing essential services to our community,' I begin, in my best imitation of Anton's authoritative, sonorous tone. My chest feels full of helium. My fingers and extremities are tingly. I end with, 'For the latest updates and resources, be sure to check our website. For any questions or concerns, please reach out to us directly. Together, let's make our community a better place to live.'

This is as much joy as killing an entire horde of Uruk-hai in perfect mode, my staff glimmering with the glory of the Valar. But before I can exhale, the phone at the desk lights up.

I rush out to take the call, which is from Leanne. Through the whirring noise of multiple hairdryers blowing, I hear her say, 'Just listening in ... A bit more off the sides, darl ... You've interrupted Classics ... *buzzzzzz* ... with the council PSA. Play the regular hour – it's on the CD that says "Golden oldies" ...' The beep of another phone call interrupts Leanne's instructions and I tell her I'll play the CD before switching over to the unmistakable rattling cough of Bryan.

'*Hack ... ekh ... kha ... kha ... hack* ... Daniel, wrong time ... *heck ... kakh* ... for the announcement ... Classics hour has to' – Bryan takes a huge, chest-rattling breath – 'Classics hour has to finish before you line up the PSAs.'

My fingers tremble as I reach for the bottom CD tray in the 90s-style JVC disc changer. This must have been how Woodward and Bernstein felt when they filed all those negative stories about the president that I saw on Channel 9's midday movie last month.

That night I can only play an hour of The Return of the King, my stress making me tense in the neck. When Mum tells me to get ready for bed, I shout back that I need to finish the entire game before returning the CD to Video Ezy. She rolls her eyes and grabs the remote, switching the channel over to an episode of *El Hajj Metwalee's Wives*. Dad is sipping tea at the kitchen bench and shouts in his own hoarse croak, 'Why you so stressed and nervous, bub?'

I go upstairs in a huff. If only they knew that my dreams were about to be flattened like the veal schnitzel Mum bashes every week. Without a good letter of recommendation from Leanne, I'm bouftek. I fall into a restless sleep.

~

Sweaty after my hurried walk from the station that morning, I arrive ten minutes late to 2SSR FM on day three of my internship. It's my last chance to redeem myself, and I'm dishevelled and nervous. My blue church shirt has become untucked, its edges flopping over the waistband.

Bryan is standing in his usual position, chain-smoking next to the demountable. 'Ah, Daniel, mind making me a cup of tea, mate?'

I get to it with the resolution of Anderson Cooper interviewing a presidential candidate. I watch him on CNN via Arab Star network, which we get on our illegal satellite dish, and I always think, Damn, this man is pale.

Leanne has already started her radio hour by the time I return with Bryan's tea in hand, two sugars and milky as he likes it. Today her hair is somehow even thinner, a brittle curtain, lifeless in the airless recording studio. I busy myself alphabetising receipts until the light automatically turns off, which it does when the sensors haven't detected movement for over an hour. Then, inhaling deeply and steadying myself to impress, I walk over to the booth.

'Leanne, hi, I've almost finished with all the radio receipts. I also rewrote some of the PSAs to read better because I thought some of the wording was clunky.'

'Oh good, Daniel, yes, tricky with the announcement yesterday – clever though – shirt out ...' she says, setting all the dials back down to zero and loading three CDs into the stacker, one from a band called the Beach Boys.

'Leanne, I was wondering if I could maybe come back over the weekend a few times and do some presenting,' I continue, my face tingling. 'I'd like to cover something about Arabs in our local community, maybe do some interviews with students, politicians, local Lebanese and Egyptian families, really get the inside scoop.' I gesture with my right hand, laying out the options like mezze.

Leanne ties her flat, dead hair into a limp bun using a thick velvet scrunchie; hands loaded with binders, she walks towards her desk and I follow.

'Yes, yes, come on Saturdays. By the way, I wanted to be a weather presenter once – three kids, husband sick, single mum – dreams change. Here's your recommendation letter.' She hands me a sealed envelope.

I force myself to work through the afternoon. Is this what Anton Enus felt like, I wonder, as he climbed up the ranks to stardom? Did he have to learn the ropes from a dying asthmatic and a woman with hair the same texture as a tea towel and a similar personality? I colour-code half-slips of paper – donation receipts from the station's annual charity drive – according to category, undoing my previous work of alphabetisation.

After lunch – a cheese and bacon roll with tomato sauce that has gone soggy from sitting out too long – I farewell Bryan. 'Thank you for all the good tips and advice.' He has a coughing fit, shaking my hand eagerly by way of response.

I read Leanne's letter on the bus home.

'A bright and promising young man with a big career ahead of him. Dresses poorly.'

How to Go Off with a Bang

My son, even if you rub your manhood against a stone, it will become erect.

My parents can't attend the ceremony for my Caringbah High School Year 12 graduation because Dad has to work and Mum is afraid of driving. Before I head off for the party, they take photos of me. Their faces are shining with happiness like a feast is laid out for the whole family. 'Mabrouk habibi,' they say. Mum kisses me and Dad shakes my hand roughly. As I leave, they tell me to 'be safe' and look at me with an expression of pride and fear from the front porch before I jump into Rita's Toyota Yaris, which I have adorned with P-plates. They shout at me to be back before eleven, and I drive off, honking as I go.

It's a classic affair: dry spring rolls, tiny party pies, sparkling apple juice and Coke, a long recitation of names, shaking the principal's hand and smiling for the camera with our certificates. My classmates and I walk out of the ceremony at the Gymea Bay reception hall with our framed graduation certificates in tow. I also have a trophy that says 'Studies of Religion High Achiever' because I really know my Old Testament, on account of my childhood fear of hell if I ever missed Sunday school.

After the ceremony, ninety Year 12 students meet on the shores of Cronulla Beach to get drunk and party; alcohol doesn't really agree with me, but I still want to feel included. It's the same beach where, two years earlier, a bunch of yobbos met with the habibs who came down from the western suburbs to shank each other with penknives and bash each other's brains out – a multicultural fun day that really went left field.

I've been excited to hang out with my assortment of Anglo classmates – nerds and a few aloof, attractive ones – for a long time, so I jump into Conor O'Reilly's car. As I plan to sip some vodka later, I think this is safer. Conor, our Year 12 captain, is Irish. His eyes are green like a four-leaf clover and his hair is dark and shiny like the mahogany chairs I see in every episode of *Dawson's Creek*. Conor smells like Lynx Jungle Fresh and the sound system in his Toyota Corolla is one of those new MP3 systems that doesn't even need a CD player. He turns up his Fatboy Slim playlist and I lean back into his leather upholstery.

'You know, I feel kind of sorry for you, bro. It's like you're Arab at home, or whatever, but when you come to school, you have to turn white. Must be weird, man.' He takes a sip out of a Gatorade bottle, which I can tell is half berry and half Absolut Vodka from his breath.

'You get used to it,' I say back, staring at the pink sugary film clinging to the hairs on his upper lip. 'In our culture, we don't really talk to our parents about girls or anything anyway.' The words tumble out.

He raises an eyebrow and smirks, then offers me a sip of his Vodkarade: it tastes like cough syrup and paint thinner. He puts the music up and the lyrics about praising somebody like he should get caught on the reverb as I sink further into the seat. My head is spinning and when I go to open the visor mirror, I can see that my eyes are red and my round, chubby face is pink.

By the time we get to Cronulla, our entire year group is out on the beach, faces lit up like the witches in *Macbeth*, circling around a fire and drinking out of bottles. I take fake sips of the XXXX Gold beer cans and Smirnoff Vodka bottles being passed around. Even though I hate the taste, my parents always told me to be polite. Tracey Rasmussen takes her shirt off and runs into the water. She comes out sopping wet. My tits are bigger than hers.

Some of the white-trash boys are shouting at each other. 'Pass it, you derro!' They play footy with an old basketball that they nickname Wilson. Bashar, the only Lebo in our year group, plants a tiny flag on a sand mound and says, 'This is for Lebanon.' Leo, who is lanky and good at geography, notes this is actually a Jordanian flag and everyone tells him to shut up.

Now it's time for a round of spin the bottle, a game white people invented because they had heaps of cheap surplus beer.

They didn't know what to do with all the extra bottles and free time, so they spun them.

Bethany, who is a bit pudgy but whose eyes are always hungry, spins first. It lands on Conor. She leans in and he pecks her on the cheek.

Now it's Conor's turn, and his spin lands on me. Tanya breaks into nervous giggles. 'Oh my God, gay.'

I'm drawn to Conor's 'take no shit, give no shit' attitude. His strength isn't just physical, it's in how he owns everything around him, how he moves through the world. I'm not sure if I want to be him or just want him. I've never done anything reckless. If he rejects me, it'll be a joke, and I'll be the punchline. But I reckon it's worth the risk.

Conor grabs me by the cheeks and pulls me close, goes to kiss me. I pucker my lips in his giant hands, pouting like a goldfish. Conor howls, eyes open in an expression of admiration and fear.

'You're crazy, bro.' He pushes me away playfully. 'He was going to do it, I swear!' Conor says.

I cackle along with them all – yeah, I'm pretty crazy, I agree.

I'm genuinely tipsy now and am pretty sure Bethany is making eyes at me, but then again she is near-sighted under her round Harry Potter glasses, so it could be a mistake. On a sudden impulse, I sidle up to her. I feel uneasy, but she takes my hand while the others are distracted and draws me to a discreet sand dune, then into the edge of the shallow waves. She sits me down and forces a bottle of sweet Smirnoff to my lips. I cough and splutter, and she moves to straddle me with her thighs, gyrating on my lap, her floral skirt damp with water and the ends of my YD chinos sopping wet and crusting with sand.

'Do you like this?' she whispers into my ear.

I nod, I smile, I feel numb inside; the cold is too deep. I remember the curfew, I panic, I run to the nearest bush. I feel my stomach cleaving to my spine and pushing up my throat. I vomit my guts out. I run back to the water, but Bethany leaves me to my shame, shaking her head.

I take last train from Cronulla to Hurstville, then drive Rita's car home to Bankstown, stopping to spew once more into a bush. Dad is snoozing on the verandah on the white deckchair in a reclined position, his head lolling to one side. His tea sits abandoned, long turned cold, the Dilmah tag hanging out of the cup.

As I try to creep past quietly, he awakens with a start. 'Why you so late? Zis is not pleasing to za Lord.' His voice croaks with disappointment.

'Sorry, Baba,' I tell him. 'It won't happen again. Those parties are so gay.'

How to Make Friends

For passage in a foreign land, even our Father Abraham whored out his own wife.

On my first day of kindy at Bangor Primary, I promised myself that I would not poop in the boys toilets. The Year 2 boys would stick their heads over the stalls and make lewd comments like 'skinny dick' or 'fatty poombah', pointing and laughing at whichever victim was trapped inside the cubicle.

The two hours before recess were fine. I had to wee but held it in and focused on colouring in my giant sunflower with yellow and orange Crayolas. Post-break, things got a little more fraught, a tingly feeling running from the tips of my toes to my butt: the telltale sign of a dookie forming. After lunch, this became a full-blown emergency and, sitting cross-legged during reading hour with the knees of other five-year-olds touching mine, I was unable to restrain the hot torpedo escaping my clenched sphincter, running through my butthole, past my butt cheek and down the inside of my inner thigh.

'Pee-yew! What stinks?' Corey Tencate said.

'Yeah, that's quite bad. What could it be?' Mrs Evans asked, rolling open the window.

But I knew what it was. And I would have a thing about poop and toilets, about when and where to release, worrying about coordinating my opportunity and finding a space private enough for a full evacuation, for the rest of my days.

~

Three months ago, I logged into the HSC portal. A few seconds, a spinning wheel on the load symbol, my ears ringing. Then I saw it: 94.2. The mark blinked before me, final and absurd. It was the wrong mark. It should have said 98: the Sydney Uni cut-off for Media and Communications. I called Dad to tell him and he said, 'That's great, bub! That's a good one!'

Floating outside myself, I thought of all those months of anxious diarrhoea, all that hope and expectation and non-proliferation treaties and Geneva Conventions and Mary Shelley and Moses Maimonides and the collapse of the Weimar Republic and the Rape of Nanking, and now it was just me and 94.2. Measly, inadequate, four marks short 94.2.

I had expected hugs, ululating shrills from the women at church, rounds of applause. Instead, I had another three weeks of anxious waiting until I could finally unclench my butthole with the confirmation from the University of Sydney admissions team that they had accepted my special consideration request due to 'unforeseeable circumstances', which I had put in when Gidoo passed. My HSC score was bumped up by a few points.

For my first day of uni, Mum has bought me a pair of black polyester dress pants and a white collared shirt. 'Very smart,' she says. 'Nadif w gameel.' The Sunday night before O-Week, she makes me do a runway walk around the family room in this new outfit, which she has matched with my good church loafers. 'Yeah, bab! Go, go! Opa, opa,' she sings with little claps.

After I finish giving Mum her runway show, I lay out my proper uni clothes on my bed, which I have carefully thrifted from the Vinnies in Bankstown and stolen from Gidoo's wardrobe. My first-day-of-uni look includes a threadbare cardigan with pictures of cats on it, old khaki slacks and my church loafers, which work for both hipsters and the Orthodox Church and exude an Egyptian uncle-like charm.

Now is my moment. It doesn't matter how I got here – I'm a first-year in the most prestigious degree available.

On the Monday of O-Week, I place a collection of old books into my Kinokuniya tote bag and look at myself smugly in the mirror. I feel smart, competent, sexy. Then I drive to Gidoo's old house in Ashfield, which is still in the family because we want to keep the equity until we can sell at a steep profit. I park the car and catch the train into the city, like a real Inner West hipster.

Arriving late to the O-Week introduction, I walk through the towering sandstone arches of Sydney Uni, feeling like Charles Ryder but looking like Harry Potter. Oxford University is cold, so heavy fabrics make sense there, but I am in sheep's wool and thick trousers in the height of an Australian summer. After having sat in the packed train, I can smell Gidoo's Old Spice reeking out of the weave.

Sydney Uni is vast, much bigger than Caringbah High. It covers hectares and is a weird amalgam of tall corporate buildings, medieval castles and utilitarian 70s storage units. In the quadrangle where the media students are sitting around the jacaranda, a chunky blonde girl in lederhosen sorts us into groups and hands us each a questionnaire that we can use to 'get to know each other better, firsties.' Her name tag says 'Rachële' and she is unironically wearing pigtails to complete her Aryan look.

Finding a circle away from the crowd, I give a sheepish grin to two brunettes sitting cross-legged in the corner and a nod to a towering brute of a bloke called Nick Jarvis, who has spelled his name out in thick, full capitals on the sticker on his chest. The girls are in skinny jeans and matching blue jumpers and have their hair up in buns, making their heads look like pineapples. Nick's broad chest is in a plaid shirt and his thighs, sticking out beneath frayed denim shorts, are each the size of my torso. I reach for one of the Sharpies, writing 'Danni' with an *i* on my name tag. Cute, I think to myself.

A prompt on the questionnaire asks, 'What makes you unique?'

Laureen, one of the brunette girls, begins. 'Well, this is super random but I'm really into 90s Green Day. Oh my god, *Dookie* totally changed my life, but then *Nimrod* came out with "Good

Riddance", and I was like, *crying*, and don't even get me started on how obsessed I was with *Insomniac*. "Brain Stew" on repeat all day.'

The other brunette, Cheyanne, rolls her eyes but Nick seems impressed, fist-bumping Laureen with a smile of approval.

Cheyanne says something about how her two dads are fashion designers and did so well with their line of couture jeans that they moved from Enmore to 'a gorgeous terrace in Redfern' and that people don't understand how chic it actually is there. 'Like people think it's all druggie dole bludgers but it's so different now, hey ... boutiques and cafes and stuff.'

Laureen says, 'So true,' and Nick is distracted by the busty cleavage of the lederhosen girl, who crouches down to the circle to check in.

'How are we going, my beautiful firsties?'

'Oh, yeah, just about to say mine,' Nick announces to her tits. 'I am mad for 80s AFL ... Mate, that was peak footy culture. Guys like Leigh Matthews and Tony Lockett were absolute units ... blokes who'd smash through tackles and kick goals like it was nothing. None of this soft-tissue recovery stuff they go on about now. They'd just tape up and get back on the field. It was pure footy – way more physical, just blokes going hard.'

We all nod profusely at Nick, who has the crisp, long elocution of a private-school boy and the outfit of a plumber.

It's my turn now and my heart is racing. I can feel myself shvitzing under my old woollen cardigan. I think about my own interests: I like hip-hop, not white rock; I have never really thought about Redfern except that it seems kind of dodgy; and my dad has only ever made me watch soccer – European football. What do I say to these white people with whom I have nothing in common?

Nick turns to me. 'So what's your heritage, mate? You Indian?'

The images of the *Kama Sutra* come flashing into my mind's eye, naked brown bodies intertwined. 'Ah, no, my parents are from Egypt,' I mumble quickly. My ears are tingly with anxiety.

'So have you ever been?' Nick asks, with his private school enunciation.

'Nah, mate, all that ancient history stuff isn't for me.' I feel my lie burning my cheeks up. If these people think I'm a nerd, they'll never accept me as one of their own. 'I'm more into politics and stuff.'

Nick nods, looking impressed. The girls are playing on their phones. I need a toilet and remember I spotted one earlier near the Law Building. Excusing myself, I run past the lavatory signs to find a row of portaloos. The reek of sewage shuts up my sphincter and I decide to hold it in.

Back at the quadrangle, Lederhosen arrives for activity two: signing up for clubs. We walk from the quadrangle through Eastern Avenue. Stalls line the path from City Road to the Law Building and Wentworth Building. I pass clubs such as the Evangelical Union and the Sydney University Liberal Club. I also see weirdly specific ones like QUEST (Queers in STEM), which is composed entirely of people with fluorescent hair and whose bodies are covered in badges that say things like 'Get your rosaries away from my ovaries'. Then there's the Epicurean Society, which is ostensibly devoted to the love of good food and wine in the legacy of Epicurus, but whose stall only offers a paper plate of Jatz and three cocktail sausages ensconced in lurid tomato sauce without toothpicks. The stall is being manned by two people, one of whom I notice two-timing with QUEST. I pass Ghibli Lovers, the Korean Society, something called X-Men Student Apocalypse and the Sydney Uni Wind Orchestra.

I hear them before I see them: clanging cymbals, low chanting, the unmistakable cadence of Coptic prayers. It's the Fellowship of Coptic Orthodox University Students. Of course it is. Because even here, in the shiny progressive university utopia, I can't escape them.

'Brother, you Egyptian?' A guy in a tonya – that white gown they wear to church – beams at me. 'You've got Egyptian hair, brother, I can tell.'

How does he know? I spent twenty minutes de-kinking my hair with Brylcreem this morning. I'm wearing an outfit that screams 'white hipster' at best, or 'old Italian guy' at worst. Yet somehow he sees right through me.

'Join us, brother,' he says, with the kind of fervour that makes my heart pound. It's like that *Simpsons* episode where Marge escapes the Movementarian cult, all white robes and smiles.

My brain screams, I'll never be like you! But my mouth? My mouth says nothing.

I take a framed picture of the Theotokos, a relic for emergency prayer, and bolt straight to a student networking event. My stomach now hurts with the pressure of needing to poop and wee, but I put it out of mind because I don't want to be late for my first student event.

Here, at least, I'm not a gyppo. In this hallowed hall of critical theory, I am free. I speak the universal language of humanities. I dabble in Foucault. I *do not* eat fuul.

A lecturer named Marc Brennan encourages all the students gathered for 'Principles of Australian Media Studies' to mingle and get to know each other. If my mum saw how thin he was in his slacks, ratty t-shirt, Vans and circular frames, she would force-feed him mokorona for a week. 'Very skinny like very fat ... both unhealthy for you,' I can hear her say. 'You perfect, Danny, in the middle,' she would add, before offering me another helping of creamy pasta.

Brennan prompts us to discuss each of our 'unique cultural standpoints'. It's some exercise in learning about how journalists can't divorce their experience from their craft.

Irish, Scottish and English; something about seeing the wall that separates Catholics from Protestants in Ireland for the first time; reconnecting with her ninth-generation Koori heritage: these are some of the answers from the two white girls and Nick Jarvis in my group.

I resist the pressure to roll my eyes so much that it gives me a headache. My bowels are on fire. My thighs are numb from rocking back and forth to stop myself from peeing. The room is getting hotter. I can feel sweat pooling in my back. I take off my cardigan, then my jumper. Sticking out beneath my t-shirt is the dreaded fanela, the undershirt my mum insists I wear at all times. The pressure is building now and something has to give.

'I'm Egyptian,' I say too loudly, so that some of the other student groups turn to hear. 'We fast from meat for six months of the year, we worship animals, I go to church twice a week! Egyptian! Gyppo! Ta7ya Masr!'

Nick's eyes are wide open. Marc Brennan looks impressed from the front of the auditorium. I hit Laureen in the face with my backpack on the way to the toilets and leave my cardigan and woollen jumper in the lecture room. I barely make it to the portaloo without soiling myself.

How to Be Born

Naked thou arrived and naked thou willst go, without a good investment portfolio.

It is the day of my cousin Matthew's christening. He is technically my cousin Layla's son, which means he is my first cousin once removed, but in our family we call everyone cousin because it's easier.

Because Layla married Hussein, who is Sunni Muslim on Fridays and a dickhead the rest of the time, the circumcision will be held at an Islamic clinic immediately after the priest performs the rite at the church. At my nineteenth birthday last week, I heard Mum say that Layla was very 'loose' in her twenties and that she didn't expect that she would become so religious or take today's baptism ceremony so seriously. It's all that Layla's been talking about for weeks now.

The church baptistry is a separate room in the cathedral, with frescoes of Saint John the Baptist. The wall has a painting of a dove descending on the head of Jesus, who has white skin and blue eyes. When Father Constantinos strides into the room in his billowy cape and robe, with a woven fabric cross hanging around his neck on a gold chain, it is with a sad announcement.

'I'm sorry I'm late, everyone. Mrs Kyriakos died this morning and her sons had a fight with the nurses at the palliative care centre because they didn't think anyone was watching her.'

Mum and all my aunties suck their teeth and shake their heads.

'It's a terrible thing not to be watched in your final hours,' says Tant Carmen, as she also said of Gidoo's death last year. Dad could not come today because he is working at the shop. He starts early, unpacking *The Sydney Morning Herald* and *Telegraph* deliveries, and ends late, logging sales from the lotto machine and cheap confectionery.

Father Constantinos rummages about in his deep pockets to remove a book of prayer. 'Anyway, here we are. Let the dead bury their own dead. Where is the little prince?'

Layla stretches out her arms to present Matthew, who is wearing a white satin gown, replete with slippers and a bow on his back. The ritual is split into four sections: the Women's Absolution, Renouncing Satan, the Liturgy of Baptism and the Immersion itself.

'Layla, habibti, as you may know, in our tradition, the mother of the child is not' – Father Constantinos clears his throat awkwardly – 'to receive Holy Communion if she is having women's issues at the time of the baptism.'

'What kind of women's issues, Father?' Despite her newfound piety, Layla doesn't seem to be getting the hint.

'He's saying that you can't eat the bread if you're on your period, babe.' Hussein shouts from the corner, where he is seated and playing Angry Birds on his phone.

Layla nods and the priest, satisfied that this is now cleared up, loops his arm around hers and walks her to the altar. This kind of fake bridal procession is what Mum has been hinting for me to make since Year 10, despite the fact that I'm currently eighteen and barely legal.

Father Constantinos erupts into the Aleyson Emas Prayer, looking like the Count from *Sesame Street*, with his hooked nose and giant gown. 'Have Mercy Upon Us O God the Father Almighty,' he croons. Then it's time for the Lord's Prayer, which is punctuated by the sound of malevolent pigs chuckling and the screeching of birds just before they shatter the glass columns on Hussein's phone.

'Our Father, who art in heaven, hallowed be thy—'

'—*WAHEEEEE!*' say the pigs.

The shattering of the glass membrane and screaming of the pigs remind me of Layla's delivery last month.

~

We were all ushered outside except for Hussein. I could imagine the beads of perspiration on Layla's forehead. The sound of plastic doors opening for gurneys to come and go being punctuated by Layla's cries as Fawzia, a midwife at Liverpool Hospital, shouted at my cousin to push the baby through her dilated flaps. Hussein yelling, 'Come on, baby, you're almost there,' and Layla responding, 'Shut up, you bastard, this is all your fault!'

Some hours later, Fawzia emerged with a baby the colour and roughly the shape of a turnip. We could all feel the suspense around the gender of the child and I held my breath tight in my chest. This could go either way – and maybe even a third, if the kid had both kinds of genitals.

'It's a boy!' Fawzia announced.

Hussein came out shortly afterwards, saying, 'Now we have someone to take over the family name.'

We found Layla collapsed against the upright bed pillow, exhausted from the strain of her labours. This was her first child and a boy: an occasion of joy. Tant Carmen took the child into her arms and started thanking all of the saints she could remember, dancing in small concentric circles as she listed what felt like a thousand names, including:

Saint Rita
Saint Marina
Saint Catherine of Siena
Anba Pakhom, the wonder worker
Anba Athanasius, the first mystic
Saint Bernardino of Siena
Saint Maximilian Kolbe

Before Layla could tell her to quieten down, in walked Father Constantinos carrying a vial of oil.

'Hi, I have a couple of deaths on the seventh floor so I'm just popping in to bless the child with some oil of chrism,' the priest said in one rapid breath before swooping down upon the child, swiping the top of the baby's head thrice with holy oil and then heading out the door like an apparition. 'See you next month for the baptism,' he shouted over his shoulder.

Conversation turned to the child's name. Mum and Dad suggested naming him after his grandfather, Abdel Youssef. Layla said that this was too depressing.

How about Habib, Tant Carmen said, after his grandmother, Habiba, which means 'loveable'. Dad said that this was not masculine enough and suggested something from the Old Testament, which has harsh-sounding names that nobody likes, including Obadiah, Jeremiah and Ezekiel.

In the end, he was named Matthew. Matthew was a tax collector in the Old Testament, and Hussein was hoping that his son would be very good with money and be able to pay less tax to the tax office. Maybe the kid would grow up to have a strong investment portfolio spread across several banks with a good return on interest. The name felt right to everyone.

Later that month, the newborn contracted bronchitis and had to fight for his breath, taking up all of Layla's time. The doctor said he should recover in a month. Still, four weeks was too long for Tant Carmen, who worried that the newborn was fighting for his soul and would end up in children's limbo, which is like hell for toddlers. It was decided that the christening would happen the next day.

~

As the baptism ceremony draws to a close, the family encircle the font like a flock of birds falling on their prey. Flickering candles cast the priest's shadow against the wall, making him loom twice as large. Turning to Layla and crooning the penultimate words of the ceremony, he swells into a great eagle. 'Dost thou renounce Satan?'

'Yes,' Layla says.

'Dost thou object to all his pomps?' Father says, pushing down hard on the plosive with his lips.

'I accept – I mean, I object ... Yes, I object.'

There's a high-pitched shrill. It's the sound of birds flying into pigs. It's a real slaughterhouse, that Angry Birds.

We pile into Hussein's '98 Toyota Tarago later, for the same-day circumcision at the Al-Ghazali community centre, where Dad meets us, having caught a train from the city after he closed the shop. 'The kid should get all his traumas at once,' Hussein suggests of Matthew's big day out.

In the back seat, after a ceremony performed by a man in a white skullcap and Fila tracksuit pants possessing no medical accreditation, Layla cradles her shrieking baby. Hussein is driving, while Mum prays the Rosary in the passenger seat. I tell Dad, with whom I'm bundled up in the back, that this kid has had a rough start. With a Christian mother and a Muslim father, he's been subjected to the traumas of centuries of religious tradition.

'Ah, habibi,' Dad responds, shrugging his shoulders. 'Life is about survival. Strangers will never stop trying to cut our dicks off and pushing our heads underwater.'

How to Make It

Or How to Play the Beautiful Game

The ball doesn't care who you are, only where you put it.

When I get together with Dad and Shoukry, we always shoot the shit. Shoukry kicks things off with his usual bluntness.

'Fareed, why didn't you do better in business? You could have been a millionaire if you'd invested in Apple.'

Dad freezes. Even the pumpkin seed shell dangling from his lip looks shocked. My eyes go wide and I take a quick sip of Coke Zero, almost choking on the fizz. This is rude, even for Shoukry.

The question hangs in the air, enough to make Dad pause the Arsenal vs. Man United match on TV. 'So you think it is very easy for your uncle?' He shakes his head, spitting out the pumpkin seed. 'You think you come and go from this nice house for free? You want to know what it's really like to migrate? See that player?' He points at a lithe figure frozen mid-kick on the screen.

'Ronaldo,' Shoukry offers. I'm glad he didn't ask me because I mainly watch the game to see the players in shorts.

Dad scoffs. 'This one here? A faffy boy, a show pony. But when I was young, in Port Said, they called me sarookh – the rocket. Go, Fareed! Run, Fareed!' He looks off distantly. 'I was strong and fit, better than Mo Salah. Back then, they all said, "Fareed, he's going places." But my father – your gidoo – very religious man, wanted me to become a priest.' Dad sighs, lost in the memory, then resumes the match on the TV.

Shoukry's gaze drifts back to the screen. At that moment, there's a close attempt on a goal. Shoukry jumps up, yelling in protest. Dad slaps the table, making the bowl of pumpkin seeds skitter sideways.

We are all drawn quietly in to the video assistant replay. A suspenseful lull. Then Dad explains that he has always had to be his family's keeper: a safety net at times of crisis. Shoukry looks at my father with an expression of tired resentment – his simple question has elicited a whole monologue. The referee announces a red card.

'They always said to my parents, "Fareed will pull his weight, help keep food on the table, instead of chasing dreams like some rich man's son."' Dad points to the mantel where a faded wedding photo of Gidoo and Teta sits. Teta's in a gown with a lace veil, looking like a frosted snowman. Gidoo's got a dashing look, like a young Omar Sharif, minus the jawline. '"At least you'll always have Fareed," they'd say.' Dad's voice softens. 'My brothers and sisters followed their dreams. But me? I was the one who got tied down.'

Before he can go on, Mum bustles into the lounge room with a basket of washing on one hip and sighs at the pile of pumpkin seed shells strewn across the coffee table. 'Go, go! Make your mess in the kitchen. Food in the fridge, yalla.' She abruptly changes the channel and settles down to fold.

We get up, and Shoukry grabs a whole roast chicken from the fridge with his bare hands, ape-like. I set out plates and we tear into the chicken, dipping it into Mum's homemade tahini. From the living room, we hear the symphonic introduction to *El Hajj Metwalee's Wives* playing on the TV.

Dad picks a bit of chicken skin from his teeth. 'We left Port Said in the night, like criminals. One day I'm on the soccer field, and the next, your teta's running out of the house, telling us we have to pack our bags. Everything we couldn't carry, we left behind when the Israelis dropped the bombs from their planes in the War of Attrition.'

Shoukry spits out a chicken bone and I flick through Facebook, mindlessly refreshing my feed.

'In Cairo,' Dad continues, 'we stayed in Uncle William's house – tiny, cramped. Your gidoo told me I needed to work, pay our way.'

'Work?' Shoukry scoffs, raising an eyebrow. 'Weren't you like fifteen years old?'

I set my phone aside, but not before taking a screenshot of my favourite page, 'Arab Parent Tings'. Something to enjoy later.

Dad sighs. 'I had never worked before, just play, play, play. But now I'm serving tea to businessmen in Uncle William's office. I'd watch them sip coffee with three sugars. This is why I don't like you working in that cafe at uni,' he says, turning to me with a pointed look. 'You should be studying, not wasting time making faffy lattes.'

Before I can push back, Dad is already lost in his story again.

'We packed everything, even covered the apartment in newspaper, all the nice sofas like French antiques. Then we drove to the airport, quiet like we were going to a funeral. I remember sitting by the window, raising my neck to see.' At this, he lifts his round bald head slightly, as if in quiet remembrance. 'And when I saw Sydney's skyline ...' He pauses, shaking his head. 'All that open space. Like a soccer field with no players.'

I glance at Shoukry, who, with his glazed-over expression, could be lost in thought, but is probably just thinking about his next meal.

'Kareem had come ahead of us, found a place in Ashfield, near the mall. It was 1969, and the 7-Eleven was an old Polish club. We stuck together with other migrant families – gyppos, Poles, Greeks. Everyone held on tight. Not like now.'

We move back to the lounge. Mum has left to scream at her sister on a Skype call.

Dad lowers his voice, leaning forward as if sharing a secret. 'They put me in Ashfield Boys High School right away. Everyone called us wogs. I didn't understand anything – no Shakespeare, none of it. But my maths was still good.' He gives a smirk at this small victory.

'I got a job at the meat pie factory in Alexandria, worked

with the Polish boys. Your teta worked in a bag factory, Gidoo did night shifts with CityRail.' Dad goes quiet, thinking of the sacrifices, I guess, but he quickly shakes it off, continuing with a hint of pride in his eyes. 'Your aunties got to go to school, to uni, but I went to the trade college, where the TAFE is now. Learned how to fix things, practical skills.' He nods, more to himself than us.

'Years later, Kareem visited the old house in Port Said. Only thing he found was one of Carmen's baby shoes, buried in rubble.' His voice catches for a second, but he brushes it off. 'One Christmas Eve, I went down the street to the Polish club. We played soccer with the other migrants – the gyppos, Greeks, even a few Aussies. And at midnight, we all walked to Sydenham, the new Orthodox Church.' Again he stares into the distance, locking his gaze onto the wedding photo of Teta and Gidoo on our mantlepiece, a young man and woman in an elegant suit and floral bridal gown, black and white – they are forever youthful. 'When the priest came out, he asked if we had thanked God for this land of opportunity.'

There's a pause, a weight to the silence. It's broken by Mum shouting, 'You have to take a break, Huda! You are not a donkey!'

Dad gives a little shrug. 'I said, "I thank God for soccer."' He looks at me and grins, like he is passing down a hard-won truth. 'So remember, bub, not easy, but in the end … it's a beautiful game.'

How to Go Back to Your Roots, Part 1: Departures

Better to eat crumbs in your own homeland than feast on bread with strangers.

At the Egyptian consulate building today, the staff are wearing ties with the Egyptian crest on them. The state eagle bears the national colours, red, white and black, proudly on its chest. Kofta meatballs with skewers running through them and three-cheese pastries with oregano are being circulated on little trays. They've busted out the good shit for today's visit from the Egyptian Minister of Emigration.

'They're never this nice when it's just us, bro,' my cousin Ayman says, staring around the main room of the Egyptian consulate in the city high-rise. The cube-shaped Mitsubishi air conditioner is whirring loudly like it's busted. It makes an uncomfortable background noise against the low mumbling of everyone present here: parents with their children who are contemplating a state-sponsored trip to Egypt.

'Bro, I swear, if I get harassed in Cairo, I'll shank the bastard,' says Rita, who talks like she's in an episode of *Orange Is the New Black*, even though Mum and Dad never let her leave the house without me.

In walks the Minister of Emigration, who the Egyptian media call 'El gamda' because she did judo at school and is one of only nine women in the entire Egyptian parliament. But it's the Chanel jacket, neat bob cut and savvy-looking eyes, faintly wrinkled at the edges, which show us that she means business.

The ambassador, a lazy man who has never lifted a finger for president or homeland, stands to attention. 'Ya hala, ya hala!' he exclaims before bowing, his tie sitting over the low paunch of his swollen belly.

'Look how much arse-kissing is going on here, bro,' Ayman whispers loudly. 'Astaghfirullah Al Azeem,' he adds, despite the fact that he isn't Muslim.

'Remember when we came here to watch Egypt play in the World Cup and all they gave us was Domino's pizza on those mouldy beanbag chairs?' Rita says to me. 'Meanwhile, this chick arrives in a pantsuit and they treat her like the Queen of England.' Rita doesn't give a crap about Egypt but she is excited about a free trip where she can do whatever she wants – under the watch of government minders.

We stand for the Egyptian national anthem. Some of the older uncles are brought to tears by it. Ayman yawns and I nudge him. 'Don't be disrespectful, you gronk.'

I don't know why I care so much about all this anyway. Mum hates Egypt, says it's dirty and unliveable, and came here with her sister when she was twenty-one because Mum 'wanted to make a better life for my children'. Dad's house was bombed in the Arab–Israeli War of Attrition, so it's not like we have any land or property to inherit.

Also, I'm pretty sure I like guys, so I wouldn't want an Egyptian wife let alone one that's my cousin, a prospect my uncle has been pushing on phone calls with me for years. 'Vevo is getting to be a young lady,' he says about his youngest daughter, my cousin Yvette. I just grit my teeth and smile through these awkward video calls while my stomach eats itself from within.

Just acting gay might get me in trouble. It would be risky to explore it in Cairo, especially after all the reports I hear about what they do to alleged homos in prison: sticking poles up their arseholes or forcing their mouths open to test which inmate can swallow a cucumber whole the quickest.

On all counts, Egypt is not really my country. Still, distance makes the heart grow fatter, or something like that, and I start thinking about how fun a trip with this group of dropkicks could be. We are fifteen early twenty-somethings who are Egyptian enough to eat molokheya, a thick green soup made of mallow leaf, but not enough to have been conscripted in the military or vote in the elections. I could go dancing at clubs in Zamalek. Eat really fresh koshari from street vendors. Ride camels at the pyramids. Sail down the Nile.

Mum and Dad's worry about Rita's 'loose' friends drains my

focus. Since it's a big deal for Egyptian girls abroad to return to Cairo on a government tour, the staff will keep them closely supervised to avoid any dishonor. That means she can live her life for a while: eating shawarma, shopping in Cairo or whatever she does for kicks without me needing to follow her constantly. Anyway, I'm quickly distracted from this train of thought by a handsome member of the waitstaff, who is dark and tall and makes me desperate to get out of my parents' house as soon as possible. This trip is beginning to look exciting after all.

Her Excellency begins her speech. 'You are foot soldiers for Egypt abroad, you carry the patriotic flame of the motherland within you and it is up to you to keep it burning.'

'Yes, Minister, but I need permission from border security to import 300 grams of hibiscus-flavoured tobacco from Cairo!' Ayman shouts.

Half the youth and a couple of parents tell him to shut up.

Then the minister invites us on a fourteen-day tour of the homeland called 'Return to your roots'. The handsome waiter, who I swear smiled at me, hands the brochures around. The Egyptian government pamphlet says:

> Come see all the wonders of antiquity, from the vast and majestic beauty of the pyramids, replete with a modern light show.[1] We will then enjoy the vibrant and sprawling markets of Khan el-Khalili,[2] socialise with military and political leaders and, finally, an inspiring and majestic Nile cruise.[3]

[1] May cause epilepsy

[2] Vendors are known to upsell tourists

[3] Gastroenteritis tablets complimentary

All the early twenty-somethings are pumped, but the parents are stressed and immediately launch into a series of loud questions. With her military training, the minister barely flinches at the barrage.

'I don't want my daughter kidnapped by Islamic State.'

'If something is stolen from their rooms, what will they do?'

'Will my son meet the president and, if so, will he replace my old passport from 1956?'

The minister arches her back and responds coolly.

'Yes, sir, we don't want your daughter kidnapped, and with God's grace she will not be.'

'Madame, the Egyptian hotel staff are mainly Filipino migrants on strict working visas, so there will be no funny business.'

'Amu, the president does not deal with visa or passport inquiries. For that, visit your local consular website.'

I fill out the form. It includes questions such as, 'Have you ever or will you ever be involved in media which is hostile to Egypt, her public image or her national interests?' and, 'Have you ever been involved with behaviour which is licentious and against Egypt's moral constitution such as homosexuality, sex outside of marriage or the use of illicit substances?'

I quickly tick no for all the boxes, write down my passport

number and text my cousin Emad in Cairo: 'We r coming next month.'

He responds: 'Pls bring iPhone chargers. Not cheap Chinese ones, proper Apple, bro.'

Two weeks later, I'm on an Emirates flight, sipping red wine from a tiny bottle and watching a censored version of *Titanic* on a small, blurry screen. The stewardesses all have orientalist red fez hats like in *I Dream of Jeannie*, all the male flight attendants are gay and Rita and Ayman are playing Temple Run on their phones. I drift into a magical sleep, flying to Agrabah with Aladdin and clutching the edges of his magic carpet.

How to Go Back to Your Roots, Part 2: Wonders Along the Nile

Do not drink the waters of the Nile, lest you contract hepatitis.

We touch down in Egypt, confused. There is already a long line of passengers standing in the visa queue. Our group, however, is ushered directly into a side office where a group of ministerial aides, who are also all twenty-somethings, are waiting. One of them, named Noor, gawky and wielding a big camera, greets us smiling.

'Ya hala, ya hala! Welcome to Egypt, ya shabab!'

Scrolling Facebook on the bus to the Nile cruise later, I see photos of us standing in a group in front of the airport looking like trolls splashed across state media channels such as NileSun. The caption for these images is, 'Youth enjoy the Cairo sun as the minister welcomes them for a state trip to Egypt'. The minister is nowhere in sight.

As the Nile is one of the few rivers that flows north, we'll fly from Cairo down to Aswan and then sail all the way downstream, against the wind, back up to Luxor. The trip to Aswan is short and smelly, an Egyptair flight where we are surrounded by men eating pumpkin seeds and wrapped in white shawls.

In the promotional pamphlet we received on arrival, the steamship *Sudan* is said to be one of the most 'opulent boats cruising down the Nile: with all the charm and Victorian elegance of Agatha Christie's famed *Karnak*'. The pamphlet also boasts about the ship's 'spacious cabins, a broad and generous deck area where locals can take in the sights, Egyptological tours, authentic Egyptian cuisine and an oriental dance night to wake the pharaohs.'

The ship is big, but it also looks run-down. Its green saloon-style doors hang off their hinges and the deck furniture is busted and old. While other boats have jacuzzis on the top deck, with scantily clad Russian tourists running out of the Scandinavian-style saunas and into the plunge pools, the *Sudan* only has one shallow above-deck spa, which is full of screaming Egyptian kids.

'It doesn't look any bigger then the *Mauretania*,' Rita says, repeating a line from *Titanic*, a movie about another boat that people ultimately regretted boarding.

We make our way upstairs to pay the fare. A sign saying 'No AMEX!' sits on the wall above the bar.

'I thought this was all expenses paid?' I ask Ahmed, who is our tour operator and Egyptologist.

'Yes, all expenses paid for access to the tour sites, but you must cover the cost of your own accommodation,' he says in a weirdly chipped American accent. 'It will be 15,726 Egyptian pounds or 800 American. Will you be paying cash or card?'

After paying, I go up to my cabin, the length of which I can walk in a couple of long strides, and lay down my bags. In the cabin bathroom, I notice a smear of shit on one of the toilet paper rolls. How elegant, I think. After a quick lie-down, I hear the low rumbling of the engine and the *Sudan* lurches forward.

It's time for lunch. The food is good and everything is served in giant tureens. There's a beef stroganoff, zucchini stuffed with mince beef and rice, and a salad bar with freshly cut fruit and vegetables, including cucumbers, radish flowers and shiny green olives.

'Don't eat those. The water will give you diarrhoea.' Ayman says abruptly in my ear.

There's also a dessert bar with small cakes, including my favourite: basbousa. Unfortunately, someone farts near the food and the odour wafts through the *Sudan*'s 'banquet hall', ruining my appetite.

Before the last fork can fall, it's time for our first stop: the temple of Philae. Nauseated from lunch, we trudge down into the temple courtyard along the planks of wood that connect the stern of the boat to the shore. We must look like the crocodile god, Sobek, our bellies bloated and our faces long.

'The penis of Osiris is here impregnating his sister-wife, Isis. You can see the penumbra of light emerging from the union of the genitals, which is the creation of the visible universe,' Ahmed says, focusing on a specific section of the vast temple facade with his laser pointer. My eyes follow the fine tendons in his fingers down his wrist and to the tattoos adorning his strong forearm.

The only way to talk about sex in public in Egypt is through Egyptology. On one of the sandstone temple walls, I notice a scene of two women wrapped in an embrace and kissing. I ask Ahmed what this represents.

'They were sister-friends,' he says.

In a uni subject called Queer Representations in the Near-East, I remember learning that depictions of homosexuality weren't completely uncommon in Egyptian culture. Ayman is wearing a black-and-white keffiyeh on top of his puffy North Face jacket, and I tell him, 'That's Palestinian, not Egyptian, bro,' to which he responds, 'Same difference, man. Yasser Arafat is my boy.'

I pass through the bookshop on my way out and skim one textbook on 'same-sex relationships of the Nile Delta and Upper Egypt'. I find a section about the two male high officials Niankhkhnum and Khnumhotep, who were buried together in the Fifth Dynasty and whose cartouche says, 'They were together in life and now they will be together in death'. Maybe they were just roommates, I think, as Ahmed shows us to the shawarma stand near the toilets for lunch.

'This is all gay as hell,' I say to Rita as our group of thirty twenty-somethings – all Coptic except for two Muslims and uniformly in North Face jackets and New Balance shoes – walks back aboard the steamship.

'Denial's not just a river, bro,' she says, scrolling Shawn Mendes' Instagram feed.

A fretful round of deckside poker begins. Some of the bros argue about whether Ronaldo is a better forward than Mo Salah. The government-appointed minder breaks out in tears, overwhelmed by the high stakes and also probably by not being paid a fair wage. He continues taking photos of us anyway. Poor Galal, I think. Fresh out of school himself and now forced to babysit thirty spoiled foreigners. He looks sad in his plaid shirt and frayed jeans. As the second of three brothers, he could be called to military service at any time, so I comfort myself in the knowledge that this must still be a pretty good gig. I watch the sun setting over a yoke of oxen. Some kids moon us as we sail past, running back and forth into the river with their arses out.

On the top deck, a guy with an afro and a statuesque bearing hands out pamphlets that say 'Ramy's full-body rimidial massaje'. The girls laugh effusively, covering their mouths and shaking their heads. The guys throw poker cards at each other playfully.

'Ayman, bro, want a massage?'

'Yeah, you gronk, you know I'd love it.'

I'm intrigued. This whole trip my neck has been sore and my shoulders tense. I lift my hand to get the guy's attention. He approaches, smiling.

'Do you have many customers on a boat like this?' I ask.

'Some of the foreign men and women like it, the Egyptians

not so much,' Ramy tells me, his broad smile brilliant and winning. He really is huge up close. His shirt is tight across the vast expanse of his chest and his biceps look carved from stone like a statue of Ramses.

'I'll take a one-hour session tomorrow,' I tell him decisively, suddenly nervous.

That's when Ahmed makes an announcement over the ship's fuzzy PA system, sounding like a soccer commentator. 'Ladies and gentlemeeeen, boys and giiiirls, it's tiiiime for us to daaance the niiight away with the queens and kings of old. Get your galabeyas and your fancy dress from the store downstairs for a night of oriental music.'

The store downstairs is stocked with cheap Chinese wares: boxes of poker cards covered with the face of Nefertiti, men's and women's galabeyas, faux gold necklaces and imitation silver anklets, as well as rows and rows of shoes embroidered with floral designs.

I select a restrained galabeya the colour of chocolate. On the disco deck, where the party is taking place, almost the entire group is made up of members of our tour – so mainly horny twenty-something-year-olds.

The beats are pumping and even a few British tourists are tapping their shoes. The playlist includes Amal Hijazi and Faudel's 'Einak', Diana Haddad and Cheb Khaled's 'Mas Wi Loli', Amina's 'El Hantour' – a song ostensibly about a horse-drawn carriage which is actually just about sex – Amr Diab's 'Bahebak Aktar' and, of course, the ubiquitous 'Shik Shak

Shok'. Actually, come to think of it, all these songs are about sex.

I need a drink. The deck bar is poorly stocked, and I peruse the Egyptian-made liquors, which include Stella beer and a whisky called Chefas: it shares the same colour as Chivas Regal but has the taste of rubbing alcohol.

In Agatha Christie's *Death on the Nile*, a jaded young woman shoots the other girl vying for her man's attention and then also shoots him in a final act of revenge. A similar game of scorned love is being played out on the dance floor tonight: Nadia, who is Sunni Muslim, is fighting with George, who is Coptic, because he looked the wrong way at Mervat, one of the other chicks in the tour group. Their relationship was doomed from the start, I think, staring out at the blinking lights of Luxor and wishing that this oriental fantasy would come to an end.

Ramy is drinking a Scotch and watching the shonky Egyptian belly dancing with a benign smile. I catch his eye and raise my glass, and he winks back at me cheekily.

The next morning I wake early for my massaje. My heart is beating fast and I feel a tingling across my skin as I walk to the studio deck. Ramy welcomes me with another one of those wide and winning grins. In his studio, scented candles have been lit and the lighting has been turned down low. He asks me to take my shirt off and show him where the pain is.

As he kneads my neck and shoulders with his strong hands, I ask him where he's from and he says Al Fayoum, a city in Middle Egypt that historians value for its lifelike cartouche paintings from the 1st century. One set of images, called 'the brothers', is a tondo of two young Egyptian men who were entombed under the sand. They both have Ramy's almond eyes and generous lips. Some Egyptologists call them 'the lovers'.

I ask Ramy if it's an easy job and whether he manages to get by. He says that he's doing it to support his bodybuilding, which is the thing he's most interested in. After the massaje, as I put my shirt back on, Ramy shows me photos on his Oppo phone of him bodybuilding. Every year he gets bigger, stronger. In one photo, his afro is slicked back with gel and the thick muscles of his thighs glisten with bronzer. He is wearing only a thin jockstrap.

He tells me that he's at my service if I need anything at all. He looks at me in the eye. I hold his gaze. 'Some of the Russian men ask for extra treatment,' he adds.

I feel a pang of sadness – and desire – for Ramy, who shows me some photos of his family and reveals that he is their sole breadwinner. He can't compete in the national bodybuilding competition until he earns enough to cover the cost of his youngest sister's school fees, and to do that he has to work long hours on boats and service the whims of creepy Eurotrash.

I ask him if he likes performing these services. He leans in and kisses me once on the cheek and then once on the lips. 'It depends on the client, but you're a good Egyptian boy and you may not be up to it.'

I give Ramy E£600 and go back to my room to scroll Hentai comics on Twitter. Sometimes myth is better than reality.

How to Go Back to Your Roots, Part 3: Supreme Council of the Armed Forces

Lo, the world's mother! Kind people, vast sands, high sun
– English invites the rort.

Their shirts are off. Their skin is oiled. They are buff and barrel-chested. This is the Egyptian police training camp and it is camper than a pride parade. In one famous YouTube video, someone dubbed the music of 'YMCA' over the footage of the soldiers standing wide-footed and shirtless on a parade of tanks.

Led by a lieutenant in a beret and tight-fitting camouflage gear, we, the children of Egypt, are invited to witness what the trip itinerary calls the 'heroism and grace of Egyptian youths' athletic prowess'.

'Soldier, explain what your brothers are doing,' the lieutenant barks.

A young man, plump-cheeked, lean-bodied and with pinpricks of fear in his eyes, responds sharply, 'Sir, we are pushing our bodies to the edge in service of president and country.'

He's not kidding. Elite squad conscripts, who enter the force at nineteen years of age, rise at the crack of dawn every day and are put through their paces. Currently, around thirty young Egyptian soldiers are engaged in a brutal-looking obstacle course.

Rita turns to Mervat and says, 'Oufft ... look at these beefcakes. Maybe we should get conscripted too.' They both laugh. There is no female conscription in Egypt, although some women are employed as military nurses and psychologists. The eldest son of every family has to serve a term of military service unless he gains an exemption. Even my depressive uncle Kareem had to do it. He once told me that he saw a friend walk onto a landmine during the Six-Day War.

The young soldiers pass under a lattice of ropes that are on fire. From this, they perform a high jump over a bush, scale some wide-set monkey bars, traverse a pool of water and leap over a quicksand pit. Then, still shirtless, the soldiers assemble and disassemble a row of guns at the 'artillery station'. Off goes the barrel and the chamber, off comes the holster, the magazine and the muzzle. These guys are disassembling huge AK-47 rifles as easily as you might fold a shirt.

'I'd be happy for him to handle me like that,' Rita sniggers to Mervat.

My uncle once told me about what military conscription is

like in Egypt. I catch sight of one of the young soldiers, the one with the pinpricks of fear in his eyes. He can't be any older than twenty-one. I wonder at the strength and heroism of these guys but also at the conditions that have driven them to this point.

They are paid a meagre stipend of E£250 a month for their efforts, which is less than US$30. Many of the boys from middle- and upper-class families bribe their way out of the institution. Those who can't are forced into the hellish and punitive routine of intense training, only to end their service with menial tasks like construction or janitorial work or, for the less fortunate, a possibly deadly stint in the Sinai. If they're very lucky, they might act as aides to high-ranking generals, but even then, they are pretty much servants who get coffee and stand guard at doors.

The same military was tasked with performing virginity tests on young female revolutionaries during the Tahrir Square protests last year, a heinous sexual-abuse tactic used to quash dissent. Even to make it into the force, soldiers themselves sometimes undergo 'homosexuality tests', where their arseholes are examined to see if they're larger than usual, in which case they are exempted. Those who are ruled out by this absurd measure have their lives and employment chances ruined by the lingering stigma of their dismissal. My sphincter tightens just thinking about it.

Finally, we make it to the office of the Minister of Youth, who is based right near the military training camp and is himself a former soldier.

We hear the rousing tune of the Egyptian national anthem. 'Beladi, beladi, beladi, lakee 7obi w fu2aadi.' The lyrics translate to, 'My homeland, my homeland, my homeland, my love and my heart are for thee.'

We all stand dutifully, following the lead of the young and handsome minister, in his lieutenant's lapel and badges. Even Ayman and Rita, who usually mumble, chew gum or roll their eyes at these events, sharpen up, looking focused and serious. It probably helps that the room is surrounded by state TV cameramen, who are broadcasting 'the minister's meeting with young Egyptians abroad' in real time across channels like NileSun and MisrToday.

Over the years, shabab el sawra, the young people of the revolution, have been alternately criticised as unruly troublemakers or celebrated as great heroes and martyrs of revolutionary fervour. At today's meeting with the minister, I'm curious to know how youth are perceived now.

That's when cousin Emad barges in. They frisked him aggressively at the front gates, but he's polite enough to kiss me once on each cheek before bagging the Apple chargers I have lugged around Egypt for him. 'Thanks, habibi. Yalla, I take you out for shisha later!' he shouts across the room as he is escorted back out by two giant security officers.

We are seated around a long table for a video presentation on Egypt's progress against 'the challenge of foreign manipulation and internal unrest'. The waitstaff bring us pastries and glasses of mango, guava and pineapple juice.

'Don't drink the juice, bro. It'll give you the shits,' Ayman hisses down the table.

The video is highly produced and polished-looking, and it begins with images of sinister men in dark cloaks and hoods conspiring around a table. Then there is footage of the revolutionaries on Egypt's streets, calling for the resignation of Egypt's former ruler of thirty years, Hosni Mubarak. They march around Tahrir Square, where a mother in a hijab embraces and kisses a young soldier. More young soldiers now, riding tanks, raiding the Sinai desert by night in the glare of infrared technology. 'Many have tried to challenge us before, but the will of the Egyptian people will always succeed. With bravery and heroism, we rise to the defence of our homeland. By God's will, we shall rise victorious!' the deep and sombre-toned male voiceover declares. I hear Ahmed, the Egyptologist tour guide from earlier, scoff and chortle under his breath. He is also one of the Minister of Emigration's aides: she really works her team hard, this woman.

All of the ministerial aides and staff are nodding vigorously except for Ahmed, and as I look closer at his wiry frame, I notice a tattoo of the symbol of the uprising: the face of Khaled Saeed, the young victim of police brutality. The phrase 'kefaya' – 'enough' – sits beneath Khaled's face. It's hard to make out, but it's all there on his wrist.

'Egypt has been through much. In a few years we will be honoured to host the Africa Cup of Nations. Just think of it, the continent's finest players coming to Cairo for this landmark event,' the Youth Minister announces in a booming voice.

'Why are we talking soccer after a video of a terrorist raid, bro?' Rita asks us.

The pressure in my chest mounts. I feel like something is about to snap inside of me.

'Minister, what do you have to say about the reports of police brutality against young revolutionaries, with some of them dying on the streets of Midan Al-Tahrir or later in military prisons?' I hear myself say, my disembodied voice floating out into space.

The vibe in the room changes suddenly. The minister's staff shuffle uncomfortably. One of the TV cameramen lowers his boom mic awkwardly. However, it's the minister's face that tells me I have overstepped the mark. He goes from loving father to angry pharaoh, his smile dropping and his eyes narrowing.

'Young man,' he begins, 'we don't only serve the elites; we are here for all Egyptians.'

I don't know if this is a very good answer but I am distracted by all of the medals glittering on the lapel of his jacket.

Ahmed approaches me afterwards. 'I'm proud of you for asking that question,' he says. He looks sad; his dark eyes have seen too much violence and too much death.

Everyone goes to enjoy the buffet lunch in the main hall.

'Bro, you really went too far with that question,' Ayman says. 'But do you have any of those Imodium tablets? I'm about to shit my pants from the pineapple juice.' He runs to the toilet while I stand alone, wondering if I could even make it over the first obstacle course in the military training.

How to Keep a Part-Time Job

An enemy's arse is warmer than a lover's cold cheek.

Another day at the Cupcake Bakery, which is touted as 'Sydney's premier location for sweet treats, confectionery and cakes galore.' Everyone loves these cupcakes: businessmen, male nurses from the Royal Prince Alfred Hospital nearby, the male hairdressers next door. In my pink apron hanging over my black t-shirt and jeans, I feel neat and tidy but also cute and sexy.

Charlotte, who seemed relieved when I first walked in and handed over my résumé for a counter gig a month ago, is now frantically folding pink twelve-set cupcake boxes. 'Yuki really should be doing this, but I had to send her to the Queen Victoria shop today because they're short-staffed.' When Charlotte is stressed out, her eyes grow smaller and her round face goes starchy, like a Coles supermarket potato that has sat out for too long. It's also in moods like this that she speaks disparagingly of Yuki. 'I don't understand why she didn't take the manager gig; she's too shy. "Sorry, sir, yes, ma'am." Honestly, Yuki, grow a spine.'

Yuki, the small Japanese woman who works with us, is extremely quick at the till and has a gentle, sweet manner. At times, Charlotte can be nice too, like a matronly aunt, her full figure and small hands deftly icing cream cheese onto red velvet cupcakes. But today she's more of a frightening Miss Trunchbull, her topknot bobbing back and forth and her voice becoming coarse and deep as she reprimands me erratically. 'Danny, I need you to pay better attention to these till transactions. I don't want Michael flagging any shortfall.'

Michael's name is enough to deflate me, my heart dropping to my stomach and eliciting a wave of anxiety farts at the mention of our franchise owner. I saw him once, walking in with his chest out and head back, his narrow eyes forming shark-like slits across his broad forehead. I saw the way Yuki, and even Charlotte, rushed about like sardines at dawn.

Still, this job has a lot of perks. You really don't know the fun of cupcake land until you gently place a dozen cupcakes into a pretty pink carton with a bow-tie-shaped cardboard handle. Honey drizzle, chocolate dream, red velvet, vanilla thriller: all of them nestled neatly together and handed over to some happy customer.

The next morning, after a bumpy ride down George Street, my spirit is renewed by a special ritual. Yuki is showing me the secret ways of the cupcake, hidden behind a veil of cream. Today, I learn how to prepare the hot cupcakes for sale.

'Daniel, let me show you how to prepare the rose syrup for the honey drizzle,' Yuki says, gloving up and donning her apron as Charlotte leaves in a flurry to check how things are going at the QVB shop. When Yuki dresses cupcakes, she does it with the precise dexterity of a preschool teacher laying a toddler down for a nap.

'Gentle, Danny, gentle with the syringe,' she says to me, cupping my hand with her soft little palm as she helps me guide the viscous sweet syrup over the still-hot cupcake, steaming fresh from the microwave. I feel like the trainee geisha from that movie where Michelle Yeoh shows her how to make a guy fall off his bike by giving him a sultry look on a Kyoto street corner.

With just Yuki and me behind the counter, I play Madonna's *The Confessions Tour* on the speaker and dance in my pink apron, folding boxes and topping chocolate cakes with cream cheese. Icing cupcakes is a huge milestone, eclipsed only, maybe, by completing the barista course. I'm happy because my favourite customer is coming in: on Thursday nights, Glenn, the head producer of Channel 7's *The Morning Show*, always swings by to get his dozen vanilla thrillers. I really want to work at Channel 7, and the only reason I'm here on weeknights is to make a bit of extra cash on the side because interning at the *Inner West Courier* doesn't pay.

'Hey, Danny, just the regular please,' Glenn shouts, all businesslike, though his voice is often singsong. He's thin and elegant with a dimpled grin and fair, fair skin, like a Shinto priest.

I ring up his purchase. The only stressful thing about this job is transactions at the till: having to carry ones and deduct tens, people never having the right change or suddenly handing me a 20c coin with the superfluous suggestion that 'this might make it easier'.

If it's $24.50 for a dozen, loyalty discount, that's $12 ... or is it $22? I wonder to myself. I feel stressed but try to seem cool and hand him a twenty. I'm pretty sure I've short-changed him.

'How are you today?' I pluck up the courage to ask.

'Babe, it never stops – Kardashian love stories, Kardashian break-ups. Your cupcakes are the one thing I can rely on,' he answers with a cheeky wink, turning on one foot with cupcakes in hand.

My stomach flutters in a way that has nothing to do with my irritable bowel.

Yuki and I jam to Madonna's 'Get Together' in our second hour of service. Madonna is crooning about how all suffering is illusory, an idea she probably got from an unaccredited 'guru' who claimed he was a kabbalah mystic. That's when Michael, of the shark eyes, surprises us with one of his impromptu store visits.

'Right, right! Plates out, chairs uneven! Come on, let's clean this place up!' he barks.

Yuki rushes out from behind the counter to see to the shop, while Michael strides into the back room.

I try to stay calm. I won't let this Shrek ruin my fairytale.

'Hmm, Daniel, I hear you're bad at the till but good with customers. Is that true?' Michael asks.

I wish I could chuck him in a garbage bag like a tray of cupcakes past their prime. 'I'm getting better at small-change transactions and I always try to keep the customers entertained,' I say defensively.

'Hmm, well, as long as you're upselling properly, that's fine,' he shoots back quickly, catching the smell of blood as he clocks a couple of customers walking in.

'Watch this, Daniel,' he says, moving in for the kill.

The two teenagers, no older than eighteen, have small bows in their hair and are quietly admiring the premium range of cakes. I can hear from the tinny murmur of a female Japanese voice that one of them is using a translator app on her phone. They're wearing Sailor Moon–inspired outfits: white knee-high socks, school dresses and plastic tiaras with crescent moons.

'Ladies, ladies, welcome, welcome. Ah, I see you're keen on the premium range of cakes.' Michael practically shouts at them.

The two girls giggle nervously. He's overwhelmed them, played his hand too hard and fast: customers need to be gently invited to purchase, not hit over the head with it.

I deftly climb into the narrow window of opportunity.

'Hello, ladies. Like chocolate? These are chocolatey times three.' I put three fingers out to demonstrate the point. 'Chocolate batter, chocolate fondant inside and chocolate icing on top.'

'Oh, chokorēto,' the girl with the translator says. 'Chokorēto is my favourite.'

A few minutes later I box three chocolate and two red velvet cupcakes, ringing them up at the counter.

As the girls leave, I turn to Michael, who is suddenly busy with the ledger. I feel brash with easy confidence – like I run the store. His face darkens. Yuki smiles at me from the middle of the store, where she is sweeping.

The next day after uni I catch the 480 bus from Burwood to the city. Yuki and I have planned to do a barista course together, and I agreed to meet her outside the cupcake bakery. I'm excited to learn how to make proper coffee, another trick up my sleeve. While on the bus, I get a call from Charlotte.

'Danny, can you hear me? I have a bad line ...' Between the bus stopping and starting and a crazy old white man who is shouting about how the Americans actually bombed Darwin, it's hard enough to hear Charlotte. 'Listen, I have some news and I have to say it quickly.'

I'm expecting praise for my choice performance last night. Word must have come to her from the big boss.

'I have to take you off the roster.'

'What do you mean? Just for today?' There's a long, drawn-out pause.

'No, we don't think you're suited for the store,' she tells me after a pause.

'But why?!' I shout, immediately launching into a defence about how good I am with the customers and how much Yuki likes me.

'Are you questioning my authority?' Charlotte asks gruffly.

The street has become swirly like a van Gogh painting. I don't know whether to scream or laugh, so instead I breathe through the sudden pounding in my head and beating in my chest while the crazy man screams about 9/11 being an American conspiracy.

I go to the barista course anyway. I don my best smile, stick my chest out and say, 'Hi, Yuki,' as I approach the shop to walk with her to the training course.

Yuki looks confused. 'Daniel, what are you doing here?'

'I'm here for the barista course,' I tell her. 'Remember how excited we were to learn how to froth the Bonsoy?'

Yuki approaches me gently, her soft hand on my shoulder. She kisses me once on both cheeks, draws her mouth to my ear and whispers, 'Daniel, go home.'

How to Graduate*

***in a dress**
***in front of your dad**

Soft hands miss the goal but close the deal.

My Asics sneakers pound along Science Building Road and into the quadrangle. The jacaranda is in full bloom and the flowers blanket the grass. All this money and they can't hire a gardener with a rake.

The sign 'Graduate gowns' leads me to a group of stalls. A size chart says 'Small to medium', 'Medium to large' and 'Large to extra large'. I duly line up behind a row of girls who all sound like they're from the Northern Beaches, their vowels long and their faces longer. 'Is Dave coming? No, he's working late, so we're going to Nobu later with Mum,' one of them says, barely looking up from her iPhone.

I text Rita. 'Hurry up. White yuppies everywhere. Do u want me to save u a seat?'

My turn, and a pudgy woman, whose name tag says 'Cheryl', sizes me up with a pin sticking out of her mouth. 'Medium for you, love. Line up to the left.'

There has only been one other time when I have worn a dress. I was five, it was pink chiffon and it belonged to Rita. Tant Carmen had sewed it for her kindergarten Sunday-school play. I longed for its pretty caress, soft folds and sparkly beauty and forced Mum to put me in the dress. It sat snugly around my waist, flowing out around my ankles. It felt like a second skin, a homecoming. I spun around in the family room, watching the folds take flight like Storm from *X-Men*. I was summoning the winds to me. Rita, Mum and Tant Carmen clapped and laughed as I shook my hips furiously. 'Go, Danny, go, go, dance dance dance. Aywa aywa ya sarookh. You're a rocket, you're a shooting star.' I was flying, I was soaring.

Then Dad walked in. His eyebrows were drawn together and he looked like the scary eagle from *The Muppets*, all shoulders and arched brow. He probably beat his chicken wives, that eagle. I felt the hot flush of shame rising in my cheeks.

Dad shook his head. 'Eh da ya Samira? Mat shaga3eesh el mowdo3!' he shouted at Mum. 'What is this, Samira? Don't encourage this behaviour!'

A sting, a sharp but blunt pain spreading. Cheryl has pinned the hem of the gown to the soft flesh of my ankle.

'Happy with that one, darl?' Cheryl asks, as a line of white law graduates forms behind her.

'Um, yeah, I guess so, but don't you think it's a bit long around the ankles?'

'Yes, darl, it's perfect,' Cheryl says absently.

I pay $90 and go for a walk around campus, a kind of last hurrah, before the graduation ceremony starts. There's the Nicholson Museum, containing an array of artefacts stolen from the Italians and Egyptians by Sir Charles Nicholson, probably during a gap year he took to 'find himself' in Mykonos. There's the stand containing a stack of *Honi Soit* magazines, the uni newspaper run mainly by white kids from Mosman. With stories on the Chinese Communist Party's influence on the student union as well as best places to picnic in Kirribilli, *Honi Soit*'s readership begins in Vaucluse and ends in Burwood – or, at a stretch, Strathfield, which all the media students call 'the western suburbs'.

Walking towards Manning Bar, I see Miso Honi, the ironically named cafe where I would buy over-dried $5 sushi rolls as students protested on the green. My stomach turned with the crunchy, refrigerated sushi rice and the pretence of performative morality while wealthy twenty-one-year-olds with dreadlocks and Birkenstocks shouted, 'Down with HECS!' and 'More pay for sessional tutors!' and 'Hands off Palestine!' My grandparents were forced out of Palestine during the Arab–Israeli War, but you don't see me walking around with my toes out.

Outside the quadrangle is the Evangelical Union stall. Their white cross is emblazoned on the black t-shirts of the Christian soldiers, who all have the dilated pupils of crusaders. 'Have you heard of the love of Jesus of Nazareth?' I once heard one of them say to my friend Zainab, a hijabi from Granville who sat Arabic and Islamic studies with me. With her fake LV bag and giant fake lashes, Zainab gave Josh or Jack one of her filthiest smiles. 'I think you mean the prophet Isa, hunny,' she answered back smartly.

Mum and Dad are standing outside the University of Sydney's Great Hall, which looks like the Chamber of Secrets, with its vast buttressed roof made of endangered native wood. The walls are high and imposing, but instead of being covered in enchanted moving paintings, there are portraits of stoic-looking white men in wigs. I had to sit an exam here once and all I could hear were the sad echoes of people's coughs and Bic pens falling.

Dad looks like a round blob in his corduroy jacket with leather elbow patches. Mum is thin and elegant, wearing a white satin blouse over a white pencil skirt, like it's my wedding day. Their eyes are huge with wonder. We drink from little champagne flutes and eat tiny salmon mousse canapés.

'These taste like cat shit,' announces Rita, who has rocked up half an hour late, her gown cinched tight at the waist against university protocol and her feet in six-inch stilettos. She eats half a salmon mousse and puts it back on the waiter's platter. Even though Rita started two years before me, we are graduating at the same time because she worked full-time for two whole semesters at Prouds in Miranda Fair, a jewellery shop that sells rose-gold earrings to white-lady pensioners. Also, she failed three subjects and had to resit them.

Rita and I see Gemma Hashem, a Lebanese Maronite girl and one of the only other wogs in our year, who is wearing a demure blue dress and white Reeboks under her academic gown. Unlike Rita, she doesn't feel the need to always be in full drag.

'Two journalists and a lawyer – not bad for five years and 100k in HECS debt,' Gemma says.

'Don't worry, babes. When I start my own practice, I'll pay yours off too,' Rita answers, tossing back her long keratin-straightened hair.

Mum clocks Gemma from afar. She has that hungry look in her eyes and sidles up to us as Rita leaves to reapply her foundation. She pecks Gemma once on each cheek.

'So beautiful, you look so pretty,' Mum says, her heart-shaped face breaking into an earnest smile. 'Are you friends with Danny? Have you been talking?'

I feel cold inside. I feel hot in the face. I know what Mum is trying to do.

'What do you mean, Mrs Nour? We talk all the time,' Gemma says.

Mum leans in closer and drops her gaze. 'Not talk ... *talk*.' Her eyes glisten with hope.

I quickly interrupt. 'Mum, let Gemma get back to her family.'

'Okay, okay, I leave,' Mum says, but not before shooting a coy wink in my direction.

I see Dad across the quadrangle talking to Professor Minns, who taught me Principles of Australian Media Studies. She stands aloof in her giant square hat with tassels. Dad's big belly stretches out over his baggy polyester pants.

'I think Mum wants me to marry you,' I say to Gemma.

She laughs. 'Aren't you gay, though?' she shoots back, tossing her hair out of her face.

'I'm not really sure,' I say, my stomach suddenly dropping into my arse. Anxiety setting in, I air-bomb my way to the graduate seats, which are cordoned off with green velvet rope like the pre-1967 borders.

The program is stacked and very boring, with an organ recital and academic procession before the actual award ceremony.

'Bro, we have to get the shahadas framed so Mum and Dad feel like their boat ride from Egypt was worth it,' Rita whispers loudly in my ear.

After the screeching organ music, there's the occasional address, which is a special speech given by a D-list celebrity. This year it comes from lefty talking head David Marr.

'This is going to be bullshit,' Rita whispers again.

'Rita, be quiet,' I whisper back, smiling at Professor Minns, who is looking at us with her small rodent eyes narrowed.

A former host of ABC's *Media Watch* and chic power-gay, David Marr begins by calling the University of Sydney Australia's 'only true university'. He also talks about finding his place in campus life in the 80s.

'I certainly wasn't a Christian,' he begins. 'I wasn't a conservative. But who *was* I?'

My mind wanders. I'm back in the family room and I'm five

years old. 'Habibi, only girls wear dresses,' Dad begins. 'You're my big man, my big boy, so I need you to act like a man, not a faffy.' Dad's eyes are concerned, drawn down at the edges. His mouth is sad. 'Okay, baba, sorry,' I say, still wearing the pink chiffon dress.

Bzzzz. Bzzzz. Bzzzz. I'm brought sharply back into reality. A few rows back I can see Dad fumbling to retrieve his phone from his huge pocket.

'Sorry, I will squeeze in here ... Sorry, can I just get in there? Pardon me, my dear,' he mumbles, swishing his XL polyester trousers past a row of tiny Filipina women. 'Are you a bloody telemarketer? If you are, I'll be very upset!'

The awarding of the testamurs begins. Honour roll recipients are awarded first, so John Adams, Liam Anderson and Eric Archer, who all happen to be former school prefects from Knox Grammar, rise to the stage.

A PTSD flashback envelops me. All the cramming I did outside the quadrangle floods to mind: *The medium is the message, so don't bury the lead. A functioning democracy requires a public sphere. The inverted pyramid structure is the cornerstone of the journalist's toolkit.*

Big as my gown is, it still feels tight around my neck. I'm getting hot under the collar. I feel trapped. I remember the time I asked for an extension from Professor Minns, who told me that it wasn't her responsibility if I couldn't get myself organised. I think about how I had to sit Media Ethics again and now owe an additional $2500 in HECS because I failed it the first time.

My mind has wandered so far that it takes me a moment to realise that Rita is up next for her group of law school graduates. 'Rita Nour, Bachelor of Laws,' says the chancellor, waking me from my stress dream. Rita bops up onto the stage, motioning to Mum to take photos. She turns once and pauses while ascending the steps, and Mum snaps a few pictures. Then, hands on hips, Rita swishes around a second time as she receives her degree and Mum snaps some more photos while everyone laughs at Rita's swagger.

I drift back into my maelstrom. So much cramming, so many closeted afternoons studying alone in the library like a mole creature when I could have been partying at Manning Bar – making out with some guy, even. What do I have to show for it? Will it amount to anything?

We are all the way to H before I come to, in time to hear my friend called to the stage.

'Gemma Hashem, Bachelor of Media and Communications with a major in Political Science,' the chancellor declares officiously.

Dad returns to his seat. The Filipina ladies' heads knock forward in quick succession once more.

'Daniel Nour, Bachelor of Media and Communications with a major in Arabic and Islamic Studies,' I hear the chancellor shout.

I walk too quickly up the stairs and almost jump onto the stage. Mum is standing and clapping. Dad's face has creased into a wide grin and he's fumbling for his phone again. I feel a jolt, the catch of fabric around my feet. I told that bitch this gown was too long. To stop myself from falling, I lift the hem and perform a big spinning turn to avoid a trip.

I am a rocket. I am a shooting star. I am a comet. I am a cloud of novae. I am flying. I am a gazelle, caught in the headlights of my dad's Samsung Galaxy camera. I am a graduate.

How to Be Saved

Swift is His mercy, swifter His judgement.

The drive to Baulkham Hills is long and exhausting. Bumper-to-bumper traffic gives way to the arid clear land of new developments, then the manicured lawns of the suburban north-west. The narrow path to salvation that requires patience and long suffering.

Cousin Ayman is in the back seat, shouting out random facts about the global property portfolio of the megachurch we're visiting tonight, and Rita is in the passenger side, applying her mascara in the reflection of her pocket mirror. I'm still not sure why we need to drive all the way to Sydney's Bible Belt when Our Lady of the Holy Cross is much closer to Menai than the elite and private North-West, but Rita is convinced that it's worth it – she's going to find a nice white boy tonight.

In the pews, where we're sweating half an hour later under the ambient lighting, the youth pastor is gearing everyone up with an impromptu prayer that booms across the speakers.

'Yeah, Daddy Lord, we see you in your house, Daddy, we hear your voice,' he croons seductively.

You'd have to be blind and deaf to miss this house of the Lord. It soars up between the cycle lanes and McMansions of the Hills, pumping out contemporary Christian rock. It's called Lighthouse Church and it's the biggest McMansion of them all.

'Yes, Lord, our hearts are yours, Lord, and you speak to our deepest needs,' Youth Pastor Derrick says to an audience whose palms are waving high in prayer like they're drowning.

Tant Suzy, my Sunday-school teacher, said that when two or three are gathered in His name, He will always answer their prayers. Then again, she used to say that bad kids go to children's limbo and will burn for all eternity. I'm also in purgatory tonight: between Rita's marriage mission and Ayman's property-expansion dreams, I'm at sea without a boat. If I delight myself in the Lord, will He give me the desires of my heart? Or will I end up like Saint Peter and sink?

The song is building to a crescendo. Pastor Derrick walks back and forth along the stage, his fine neck and strong muscles well defined under his t-shirt.

What do I think of all this? Do I still have faith? These days, the iridescent God of my childhood seems a vague memory. I was taught that the Lord, Jehovah Jireh, was a great provider. But the only things He's provided me with are no job, no partner and $50,000 in HECS debt.

'What does God want for you?' the pastor asks. 'What's His vision for your life?'

Since graduating last year, I've been floating aimlessly and asking the Lord Jesus to help me find a good job in journalism. I am desperate for a career opportunity, my big break.

'I want to anchor *SBS World News*,' I pray to God, or Spirit, or the universe, or nothing at all. Maybe if Mum and Dad see me on the news every night, it will stop them from asking me why I didn't study law, I think.

'What stirs you? What moves you? What gets you going? That's where we're starting tonight: with a question!'

Ayman nods at the pastor and Rita is smiling at the row of guys behind us, one of whom winks back. I feel a mounting unease.

'God is stirring something in your heart. What gets you out of bed in the morning?'

I look to my left to see Rita making dry-retching noises, pretending to poke her finger down her throat, her eyes glazed over in boredom now that the boys behind her have resumed paying attention to Pastor Derrick. To my right, Ayman's eyes are focused in earnest. He is leaning forward and his Nike TNs are crossed beneath his chair.

'Uh-oh,' I warn Rita, tilting my head in Ayman's direction. 'Looks like the Spirit is taking him over.'

'SHUSH!' We get silenced by a white girl behind us, her head shaking in judgement. We have punctured her ecstasy and she returns to it now, eyes closing as a dumb grin spreads across her face.

'Bro, what are they smoking here?' Rita whispers violently into my ear.

I roll my eyes in agreement but my heart isn't in it: actually, I do want God to answer my prayers and to intervene, to make my life easier.

'Let me be a success, let me be normal, bless my family,' I pray, surprising myself.

The collection plates get sent around. A few years ago, this church was involved in a money-laundering scheme that was plastered all over *A Current Affair*. The episode was called 'Embezzled into Salvation'. We're Orthodox, so we prefer our corruption behind the altar, but with this lot, it's right in your face with the shiny suits, expensive recording equipment and ducted air conditioning.

Ayman tosses a $2 coin into the collection basket, which is unexpected because he once asked for change from a Salvation Army collector at Parramatta station.

Pastor Derrick now moves to the closing prayer, the altar call: the moment of grace is upon us. 'You're a quiet church! Give me a smile!'

I smile. I clap. Something is softening in me, some hard stone of resistance is being worn down and washed away by this onslaught of grace. The river is flowing.

'Are you ready to receive the gift of the Spirit?' he shouts. 'Come as you are! Just as you are!'

Synth music seeps out of the speaker. One by one, people rise from their seats, drawn by an unseen force. Dozens, then hundreds of guys in white singlets and floppy Havaianas and girls in frayed denim shorts are pulled forward by faith. Like files to a magnet, they march up to the altar, a shiny stainless-steel table with a big neon cross on it.

I turn in slow motion as if to ask for help, but it's too late – I'm caught in this rip-tide. Out of the corner of my eye, I see Rita's mouth agape and Ayman smiling and nodding, for I too have been taken downstream and am walking down the aisle to join the multitude of sinners awaiting their miracle.

'Kneel before the altar of the Lord,' Pastor Derrick commands, hands outstretched above the neon cross. His shirt is even tighter up close. The tears start coming. My cheeks are wet. My knees are sore. Is this me? Is this a possession?

Prayers blend with the soft murmur of the congregation, rising like incense towards heaven. Confessions spill from trembling lips, mingling with tears of repentance and sighs of relief. I can hear some of these prayers clearly – 'Save my sister', 'Bless my baby' – but others are more vague, using the mysterious language of Spirit that knows no translation: 'Sham a lama a ding dong, sham a lama bling!' Tant Suzy said that talking in tongues is a made-up nonsense, but I'm too far gone to care. Who am I to yuck their yum?

The river is cresting into a vast sea and I am lost, surrendering all.

'God, lead me. I know I haven't spoken to you in a while but I'm lost. Please show me the way.'

In that sacred space, in the embrace of divine love, I await the words of absolution. I long to be washed clean of my sin and shame, to be remade and reborn. A moment of quiet stretches into eternity. I see the pastor's lips move after I hear the words in my ears.

'Will you become a lifelong donor of the Lighthouse community by making twelve easy annual payments of $59.99?'

How to Get Ripped

You may bring a donkey to the brook, but if he refuses to drink, better to shoot him!

'Hey, bro, you're looking good – for a little bitch,' begins Djovic, my Serbian trainer. For three weeks now ahead of cousin Shoukry's spring wedding, Djovic has been taking me through a regimen of physical training accompanied by verbal abuse every morning.

Djovic says things like, 'Squat like you mean it, you little pussy!' and, 'You call that a bicep curl? No, NO, NO!' It's not Djovic's shouting that stings most, though – it's my own wounded self-esteem. The mere sight of my growing love handles, which have emerged like weeds in a garden, are a cause of personal disgust and disappointment.

On social media I am bombarded with images of lean, fit men with the body mass indexes of young greyhounds or thoroughbred racehorses. I go to Djovic because I know, just by looking at his dead shark eyes, that he can get me the results I need.

Djovic, a compact, pale man with thick calves and broad shoulders, was all smiles when he sat me down to take my bank account information last month. I was shocked by how much he charged for a three-month training contract.

When I asked if there were other, maybe less costly, options, Djovic promptly said, 'Well, of course I could see you less often and maybe have shorter sessions ... but it depends on how much you want it, bro.'

The contract ended with three 'promises'. *Yes*, I will train three times a week. *Yes*, I will commit to a strict keto diet of high protein, coffee butter 'shots', which I should drink down every morning, and no starches, especially after 7pm. *Yes*, I will commit to the discomfort, knowing this is the start of my trans-*growth*-nation. I signed on the dotted line.

Djovic has organised my workout routine into three distinct days.

Day 1 is machine leg presses, leg press calf raises, seated cable rows and seated dumbbell shoulder presses.

Day 2 is seated machine shoulder presses, dumbbell overhead tricep extensions and an elbow plank.

Day 3 is barbell back squats, bent-over rows, mid-grip spoto presses and leg raises.

The kilos drop quickly. I go from 78 kilograms at the beginning of training to 73 kilos after our first month. It's agony at first but I relax into it, finding a rhythm and riding Djovic's momentum. But as the second month sets in, I begin to plateau and stop seeing such exciting results.

At the start of today's session, Djovic measures the thick protuberance of fat off of my ribs with a plastic clamp, and shouts, 'It's time to change up your routine.' That's when we shift gears and it becomes all about high-intensity training in short-interval spurts and a strict protein diet. My eyes are full of heaving chests and strong biceps, the kind I see on my 'men's fitness and training' Pinterest board, and my belly is full of chicken breast.

Along with fitness advice, Djovic also offers life tips. 'You doubt yourself,' he tells me after I fumble a chest press movement. I say that I've been feeling a cold coming on lately and he suggests that I look up the fitness guru Wim Hof, a Dutch motivational speaker and extreme athlete known for his capacity to withstand freezing temperatures.

In the next session, I tell Djovic about all my mum's failed attempts to hook me up with a girl and he tells me about his first failed marriage. I tell him about my dysfunctional family and he tells me about his father's funeral. I tell him about my struggles to get full-time work in journalism and he tells me about the personal development conferences that he runs in the city.

One session, I ask Djovic how he got to be this way: so strict and disciplined. His eyes become thoughtful and wide for a moment as I pant between seated shoulder presses. He tells me that just after the fall of the Iron Curtain, when Djovic's father brought his wife, mother-in-law and a five-year-old Djovic to settle in Sydney's Inner West, he received some tough advice: 'Son, life very hard, but you must be harder.' Djovic says this in a thick Eastern European twang that sounds like a kransky sausage frying in a copper pot, his face brimming with pride as he recounts his father's ingenuity. Then he shouts at me to 'lower the barbell slowly' and I snap back to reality.

But despite all the positive self-talk and motivational advice, I notice that Djovic seems pretty pissed off a lot of the time. When I get haemorrhoids and have to miss two sessions, he says, 'Sickness is all in your mind.' Another time, when I am late to the gym because I was getting my flu shot, he says, 'If you die because of that poison, it's your own bloody fault.' This continues well into my third month of training, which is also when my body begins to change. I am looking more svelte, with a higher, rounder bottom and flatter belly.

Workouts are hard enough, but seeing Djovic at the gym also causes a quickening in my heartbeat and a fuzzy feeling in my head. I notice how swole he is, his biceps burgeoning underneath the tight openings of a black muscle shirt and glistening with perspiration. I try to focus on training but find it hard to avoid his gaze. He breaks my reverie when he shouts, 'Push!'

~

Cousin Shoukry's wedding is held at Our Lady of the Holy Cross. The priest offers the congregants holy bread after the ceremony. I refuse. Who needs all those carbs, I think to myself.

At the reception party, at which I am emcee – on account of Shoukry not wanting to pay a professional – I announce, 'Look at the beautiful bridal table. Isn't the bride glowing? The bridesmaids are looking lovely too.'

In truth, all I see are their thick cankles and wide thighs, the rolls of fat that come out of the top of their tight corsages. Afterwards, when I look at the Instagram photos of my dancing, all I can see are my own thick thighs and all the areas that my pants are pulled tightly across. That night, I dream of a workout that does not end.

Djovic and my body. My body and Djovic's. He taunts and rewards: he pushes me in a dance of deprivation and gluttony. Binge and purge. Indulgence and restraint. All culminating in a blossoming manhood and a tough exterior. Like a greyhound. Like a racehorse. Like a kransky sausage.

I text him the next morning. 'Bro, I'm really sick today and can't come in. Might be bronchitis.'

Djovic texts right back. 'Okay, bro, are you sure it's not just in your head?'

The more I look at my body and the more people tell me how good I look, how fit I am, how hot, the more depressed I become. After a week of lies and excuses, I break the news to Djovic over text.

'Bro, I don't think I want to train anymore 😢. I'm really grateful for all that you've done, but I can't keep this up and I need to move on. 🙏'

Djovic calls me straight away. I can't bring myself to answer and let it ring out. I furiously masturbate under the sheets and fall asleep.

~

It has been six months since my last session with Djovic. Now he runs his own fitspo brand with an activewear line that he sells mainly through Instagram. His business conference tours have become pretty famous. 'Surplus and synergies', 'Grow your business and your biceps' and 'Core strength for brand development' are just some of the titles in his training course.

I do yoga on Tuesdays and try to drink more water. My love handles have returned and I'm okay with it. I often think, with a sick thrill, of Djovic screaming at me. 'This is too much, Djovic! This is too much!' I say in my dreams. I wake up dripping wet.

How to Succeed in Politics

Or How to Be a Big Man

The leader of the village is the servant of all.

I've always been intimidated by Shoukry. Not only because he's always stood a foot taller than me, but also because he would punch me hard in the shoulder if he thought I was out of line.

Once in Year 8, after his class had to do a close reading of George Orwell's *Animal Farm,* he told Mrs Granger, 'If I was on that farm, I'd partner with the most powerful pig to police the other bitch animals. I'd shoot the horse and eat the chickens myself, miss.' He was tall, lithe and graceful then. There was strength in his forearms, beauty in his thin waist. He was like Hermes or Adonis, fleet, bright and strong.

When Mrs Granger summoned Tant Carmen and Uncle Kareem to complain that Shoukry was being disruptive in class and having violent ideations, they insisted she was in the wrong.

'Why is my son reading animal books like a faffy boy, anyway?' Uncle Kareem asked. 'He should be doing more maths!'

Later, Shoukry spread a rumour that Mrs Granger showed him her cleavage in free period and told him that she 'always liked Arab boys'. She resigned that year in disgrace and he was nominated school captain, in part because all the teachers were afraid of what he might say about them.

In Shoukry's HSC year, we all sat down for a family movie night. We were watching the scene in *The Godfather* where Bonasera comes to beg a favour of Don Corleone on the day of the Don's daughter's wedding.

As Marlon Brando menacingly lamented his guest's disrespect, face swollen with hurt pride and cheeks packed with tissues, Shoukry was lost in rapt attention. When Bonasera and the Don struck a deal, Shoukry leaned forward. My cousin's thin jaw reeled backwards towards his neck; Brando's jutted forward. Shoukry's eyes were narrowed and squinty; Brando's were wide and contemplative. Shoukry twitched and squirmed, reaching for the remote quickly to pump up the volume; Brando was as placid as a lake, barely moving at all.

Over the next few months, Shoukry became completely obsessed with *Godfather* paraphernalia. He hung a *Godfather* movie poster above his bed, with Don Corleone smoking a pipe and looking at you from behind the table with a smoking gun. He wore a t-shirt with an image of Michael Corleone holding Fredo's face and the words, 'I know it was you, Fredo ... You broke my heart.' His most prized possession was a whisky tumbler engraved with the line, 'If by chance an honest man like yourself should make enemies, then they would become my enemies. And then they would fear you.'

Shoukry went down the rabbit hole of mafia content, exploring the chummy relationship between law enforcement and Mafiosos and becoming especially interested in the position of 'consigliere', attorney and trusted adviser to the Don. He spent his nights streaming crime dramas: *The Sopranos*, *Law and Order SVU*, *Goodfellas*. Shouts of 'goomah', 'goomba', 'gabagool', 'bada bing' and 'pasta fazool' punctuated the nights like gunshots.

None of us were surprised when Shoukry said, 'I'm sitting Law at Sydney Uni. It has to be Sydney or I won't get any respect.'

He had grown bigger by then. His eyebrows were thicker and his jawline strong. There was power in his broad shoulders and the strength of a coil ready to spring into action in his firm glutes and narrow waist. Though he fell ten points short of the admissions cut-off, Shoukry scraped into his Bachelor of Laws by organising a special meeting with the head of admissions and explaining how much he wanted to be a role model for young Arab men and chart a path in the legal profession. Also, believing that the man was a 'faffy', he flirted with him a bit by complimenting his suit and winking a lot, which he later professed 'sealed the deal, bro!' Uncle Kareem slaughtered a lamb from the farm over the Christmas holidays to celebrate.

I slept over at his place that Christmas Eve and we had to share a bed. How excited I was the next morning to see him wake. My heart raced in my chest as I anticipated him stirring. I pretended to sleep. To hear the sound of his soft breaths. To hear the heaving of his chest and to feel the warmth of him radiating across the bed. His fine arms and legs, his long lean body against my short pudgy one. The smell of him, that musky odour of sleep against the old wool of Tant Carmen's thick, plush blankets with the peacock and the tiger on them.

When he spoke the first words of the morning, they came out as a raspy croak. 'Stop staring at me, you gronk. Don't be a little bitch.'

I didn't want to be a gronk if Shoukry thought that was bad.

It was on campus that he joined the Sydney University Liberal Club or 'Young Libs' for short. 'They're all white-trash pooftas, bro, but their dads are filthy rich. I gotta get to know these bastards, you know, act like one of them.'

It took him a while to convince them that he wasn't Muslim, but he eventually ingratiated himself enough to join their ranks. He changed his Fila tracksuit pants for Abercrombie slacks, his Adidas jumper for a Ralph Lauren polo and his Champion bum bag for a box of Marlboro Reds or, on Catholic Society ball nights, a smoker's pipe wrapped in a red handkerchief with white polka dots.

A few weeks after his graduation, he had his first placement as a paralegal at Smith, Jones and White, where he was known to be a precise adviser and soon enough was admitted as a lawyer. It didn't take long for a stream of clients – men and women claiming to be victims of exploitation by their bosses – to flock to his office, having been informed of his ability to 'get their rights'.

On one of the days that I visited him in court, his client Mr Ali, a slightly overweight Syrian man in a neck brace, was sitting in the witness stand. Mr Ali appeared drained, his face etched with worry, his mouth a grimace, but his eyes were shining with hope.

'Look at him, your honour,' Shoukry motioned towards Mr Ali. 'My client has been robbed of his health, his livelihood and any remaining vitality or charisma.'

Mr Ali picked his ear, blinking passively.

'A ruin of a man!' Shoukry shook his head, distraught.

'Let's not get carried away, counsel,' the magistrate said.

It was during his first year at Smith, Jones and White that Shoukry met Amal, a peroxide blonde (brunette) with great teeth (Invisalign) and a (un)naturally big arse. After a Sicilian destination wedding where he took photos on the same hill that Apollonia, Michael Corleone's first wife, exploded in a car bomb, Shoukry returned to Sydney to begin his 'side hustle'.

By opening a preschool run not by qualified childcare workers but the women volunteers of his church Sunday-school program (who Amal paid cash-in-hand after mass), he was able to have the 'safety net' that would allow him to pursue his lifelong dream: politics.

There was not a community organisation or concerned citizen who Shoukry turned away during his campaign.

During a discussion about the merits of same-sex marriage, Shoukry, who was known to swing both ways if he drank enough at Catholic Society balls in his second year of uni, met the GLBATA (gay, lesbian, bisexual, asexual, trans alliance) to promise he would show up for them at a pivotal time.

'Many of my friends are gay,' Shoukry began. 'I mean, don't get me wrong, I still think it's disgusting. You can't rig a stick-shaft without a hole somewhere, am I right?' At this, everyone stared blankly back at him. 'But I'm definitely ready to compromise. I mean, why shouldn't you be allowed to marry and be as miserable as the rest of us?'

But at the first sign of support from the local Liberal caucus spearheaded by Father Constantinos, Shoukry backflipped.

'Habibi, how can we let them marry?' Father asked. 'It would ruin everything, bring our faces to the dirt in shame. We fled our motherlands, conflict and war. But now you'll have us doubting if we made the right choice.'

Shoukry nodded rapidly. 'Yes, Father, we have to think of the children. I only talk to those people because they will sue the church if they accuse me of discrimination.' Father Constantinos blessed Shoukry and went to reallocate donations from the Sisters of Providence to a private 'discretionary funds' account.

Shoukry met with the Turkish Gallipoli Association for an Iftar dinner and with Greeks United on Anzac Day. 'They're not trustworthy,' both Mehmet and Costa said about the other. Shoukry nodded and separately slapped each man on the back as he left. 'We understand each other, brother. Blood is thicker than water, and I thank you for the vote.' And when Mehmet and Costa accidentally met in the hallway, Shoukry just said, 'I'm learning the tactics of the enemy.'

After Shoukry won his campaign by a landslide (it helped that I had defaced all the posters for his Labor Party counterpart, Chen Yu, a single Chinese-Australian mother of three who was also a nurse, and whom Shoukry had defamed as a Communist Party insider), he turned his attention to the most important pastime of all: construction projects. He waved through dozens of delayed housing development applications, and by way of example, he added a duplex to the back of his own home. By transferring funds from community donations to his personal account with the description 'private gifts', Shoukry was accruing, slowly but surely, a huge debt with the ATO and committing several acts of fraud.

'I lead by action, brother,' he told me two years into his term of office as I swam around his huge pool, which was heated by jet streams and also had a waterslide that connected from his verandah.

Watching his little ones, Kirollos and Mark, splash around, I asked Shoukry how he could afford all of this on a local councillor's salary.

'Just hustlin', bro,' he assured me, heading inside to take a phone call from his accountant.

All of Shoukry's legal woes eventually caught up with him. On the way to one of his construction sites, Shoukry swerved abruptly on the back of his Vespa as a cement mixer pulled up short in front of him. He saw it too late, shouting, 'Fucking bloody stupid shonky Chinese workers!' as he flew off the bike and soared through the air like the illegal fireworks I had seen him detonate during so many backyard New Year's parties. He hit an electrified fence, which he had had installed to 'keep all the bloody council stickybeaks out of my business'.

Shoukry finally came to in the emergency ward of Liverpool Hospital, a facility he had defunded to build a three-tier car park and rooftop members-only gym months earlier. His bones were broken in nine places, and his face was in a cast and jaw in a wire. He did not recognise the face staring back at him. It was not Amal's plump lips that greeted him, for she had left him after discovering text messages to Candace, the girl in accounts at his 'charity', but the hard features of Bill, an ASIC investigator who, having heard about Shoukry's unscrupulous property dealings and investment portfolio, handed him a formal notice of investigation.

Shoukry, who could only communicate in grunts and moans, gestured through his swollen features for a pad and pen. He wrote: 'If by chance an honest man like yourself should make enemies, then they would become my enemies. And then they would fear you.'

How to Buy a Car

Do not throw away a rotten pear; turn it into jam.

I was nine when Dad first gave me the advice that would be a golden thread, a parable of wisdom conveying all his hard-earned knowledge in a few words. He had just finished a long week at the mixed business, and we were at Menai Marketplace for a very special purchase. I was desperate for a PlayStation 1. I pointed at the Big W price tag and asked, 'Dad, is this expensive?'

He said, 'Nothing is expensive for us, but you need to get good marks in your tests.'

We went to the counter. The saleswoman was a blonde middle-aged lady with a blue name tag and her hair up in a black velvet scrunchie. Her name was Cheryl, or Jess or Mel.

'Now, tell me, my dear,' he began. 'Is this your best price?'

I went outside to let Dad work the trade.

'Why do you always do that?' I asked him on the way home, PlayStation in tow.

'What do you mean why, bub? Always bargain! Never be afraid to bargain! If you don't ask, you don't get!' Dad shouted back.

Dad has been putting this maxim to the test every day of his life. In theory, it might sound like some lofty invocation to courage, to tackle every challenge boldly. In practice, it's the more banal reality of him asking the guy at the Aldi counter if there are any further reductions on liquorice bullets.

In 1999, Naughty Dog, the company behind the PS1 game Crash Bandicoot, released Crash Team Racing. It was a timed go-kart contest based in the world of the mischievous marsupial. My sister would select the character of Crash himself or the deranged, straitjacket-wearing kangaroo, Ripper Roo. I, on the other hand, would opt for Coco Bandicoot, who was pretty and lethal with her pink tank top and jaunty updo.

I loved the way the controller felt in my hands. I loved the sounds of the engine revving, I loved the vibration coursing through my fingers and wrists as I would crash into my sister's go-kart. Sometimes I played for so long that blisters would form on my thumbs. Our family doctor told me that I should play less and go outside more.

~

I follow Dad into Volkswagen Leichhardt. He is now hunched with his sciatica, but almost twenty years after the release of the

PlayStation 1, he still has a purposeful confidence and a rugged but wearied charisma about him.

He wants me to feel satisfied with a purchase that will make me proud for a long time after I drive away. He also thinks I'm stupid with salespeople, liable to say and pay too much.

There is only one car we're really interested in, and it's not even a Volkswagen. 'European cars, too hard to maintain,' Dad says. I give the game away almost immediately, spotting the 2004 Kia Cerato, which he discovered after extensive digging online, parked outside with all the other pre-owned vehicles.

'Wow, it looks great. Seems like the last owner kept it in good shape.'

Dad pulls me aside abruptly. 'Mish t2olhom en el 3arabeya 3agbak,' he says. 'Don't let them know you like the car.'

Now that we're inside the dealership, Dad begins his predatory shark game. His face is graven in stone: vague curiosity, with little expression. He circles the gleaming, air-conditioned lot. With his walking stick, he hits a hub cap here and strikes a bonnet there. He is declaring his presence to the dealership.

In his home city – El-Qantara el-Sharqîya, a small town on the Suez Canal – fishermen would throw their lines into the canal and wait for hours for fish to take the bait. Today, Dad is also baiting his catch, deliberately provoking the sales staff – standard-issue white guys in navy-blue polyester suits. Who is the hungriest fish?

I follow him from afar, swallowing my frustration and preparing myself for a drawn-out pursuit. After about ten minutes, someone approaches. His name tag says 'Luis'. His eyes are black and beady, his teeth small and sharp, and he has a thin, slight frame. He is a sardine and today Dad will slow-roast him over burning charcoals.

'Yeah, hello there. I'm here with my son and we're looking for something small and reliable today. Now, this Kia here. What do you think of it, matey?' Dad asks skinny Luis outright.

'Well, it doesn't matter much what I think of it,' Luis shoots back. 'It matters how it feels to you, sir.' And with this, Luis opens the Cerato's door and gestures for Dad to sit down.

Dad lumbers laboriously into the front seat. He examines the freshly detailed interior. The steering wheel, the rear-view mirror, the glove compartment. He glances at the logbook. Nothing escapes his gaze or his barrage of questions about the previous owners, registration dates and thoroughness of the last service.

Dad pulls the car out onto Elswick Street. I'm in the passenger seat and Luis is in the back.

'Mr Nour, we can't go past fifty in this zone,' Luis says. Dad puts his loafer down hard on the accelerator.

'Acceleration a bit slow,' Dad says as he charges down a shopping strip, causing a small Asian lady to jump back from the pedestrian crossing and knock over her fabric wheelie trolley.

We arrive back at the dealership. Luis' composure is intact and Dad's face is like a slate of old granite in the Valley of the Kings. But I'm anxious with the possibility that I will not take this car home today because Dad won't like the price.

'Mr Nour, as you can see, this car is in great condition and I'm wondering if you would like to drive off with it today,' Luis offers.

Dad mumbles some protestations about the condition of the car. That's when Luis surprises me.

'Sir, I won't waste your time if you don't waste mine. There are plenty of other buyers interested in this vehicle. If you don't like it, please tell me now and I'll see you out myself.'

This skinny boy is no sardine. He is a Nile perch. He is made of firmer stuff than he looks. We learn later that he's from Donnybrook, about 200 kilometres from Perth, which, like Dad's home town near Port Said, is the lesser town to a more famous city. My father and Luis have some things in common. Both men are hungry, both appreciate the value of a dollar and both have nothing else on today.

'Now, Luiy, I didn't say that,' Dad says, assigning the new nickname as we sit down at Luis' desk. 'It's a good car and we're interested. We just need a fair deal.'

Dad starts listing a series of extenuating circumstances that he thinks might sway this austere salesman to our favour. They include me having a 'perfect driving record' and being able to pay in cash today. I was suspended for speeding twice and the only thing in my wallet is an expired Medicare card.

Luis still looks unconvinced, his dull eyes like puddles and his pockmarked skin like an overdone fishcake. That's when Dad reveals his juiciest bait.

'We also have a good car for trade-in,' Dad announces. 'Here's the key, Luiy. You can go and have a look.'

Luis, eyebrows raised, takes the key and trudges outside to look at my sister's 1999 Toyota Yaris, which I've been driving for five years.

A few minutes later, Luis returns with his manager, a pale man with a big belly, square jaw and red face. If Luis is a perch, this man is a red snapper. Dad leans over to me with a warning. 'He's going to say some bullshit about what's wrong with the car.' Sure enough, Luis says that with the 'thumping noise' emitted by the gearbox, the scratches to the exterior and the age of the vehicle, they can only offer a deduction of $2000 on the asking price.

Dad scoffs at this. 'You must be joking, mate!'

Tony, Luis' manager – a man of quieter gravity than his yappy protégé – speaks up. In a bellow like a ship's horn, he tells Dad that he can see how serious we are about making a purchase but that with all these liabilities in mind and the state of the market, he can't go any lower without losing money for the dealership.

My heart drops. The sound of an engine revving in the company car park ignites a vision: a countdown timer appears before me. *3, 2, 1, race!* The wind rushes against my face. The road is bumpy beneath me. My thighs straddle the seat, and the heat of combustion warms my furry arse. My snout is long and ends in a small, wet nose. I reach up to whip the yellow hair out of my face, which is held up with a blue scrunchie. This black Kia Cerato is my go-kart and I am racing to win. I turn to my father, my eyes pleading. I'm on the verge of tears.

'I'm afraid $14,500 is the best I can do, Mr Nour,' Tony says.

'Tony, my son will shake your hand today on $14,000,' Dad responds.

This is all too much. My head feels light and there's a catch in my throat. I need a break. I go to make a cup of coffee at the courtesy De'Longhi espresso machine.

When I come back, I find Luis grinning his crooked smile and Dad chuckling softly. Something has changed between these two men. The real arbitration, however, is between Dad and Tony.

'I can't budge any further, Mr Nour,' Tony declares wearily, his face a mask of exhaustion. 'It's $14,200 or nothing,' he concludes, followed by a weighty silence.

Tony looks at Dad. Luis picks his teeth. Dad turns to me seriously, with his eyes wide in a questioning stare. He has fixed the contest, but mine is the deciding vote. Will I accept the terms?

I reach forward to shake Tony's hand.

After a half-hour session of contract-signing and payment transactions, Dad stops on the way out, looking to see if I will say anything else. I surprise myself.

'Luis, can you throw anything else in to sweeten the deal?' I ask, and Dad laughs.

I drive off that day with a new car, two umbrellas that say 'Leichhardt Volkswagen' and a feeling that I have just won a time trial in perfect mode and finished all my homework.

How to Break News

Better to slip through a truth than be caught in a lie.

The arbitration trial at the *Daily News* head office is fraught. The walls of meeting room 4, which is called 'Gadigal', threaten to close in around me. The fluorescent office lights blink down in judgement and the ducted air conditioning whispers 'liar' in a grating tone.

Seated on one side of a table as we review my termination papers, I'm sandwiched between Janette, the HR legal partner on my left, and Barclay, my hiring manager on my right. I'm like the bacon in an egg roll, which is the nicest part but also haram.

'So you're aware that our organisation considers copyright infringement a fireable offence?' Barclay asks, his voice raspy from too many Winfield Blues.

'Yes,' I pout, my eyes downcast and my head swimming.

'And you admit that when we notified you of the complaint from another newspaper for whom you first wrote the story, you responded' – at this, he clears his throat – '"I knew in my heart that clicking publish was the wrong thing to do, but I felt it was necessary to get ahead"'.

This time I just nod, tears stopping up my throat and white noise blocking my ears with shame.

'Well, in that case, we've no choice but to let you go. Please gather your things and leave immediately. I'm sorry, we thought you had a promising future here.'

My stomach shrivels against my spine, my heart drops into my arsehole, but I say nothing. I walk back to my desk to gather my things while hundreds of others clack at their keyboards or make calls to the PR team at Foxtel to get the latest scoop about the Real Housewives of Melbourne's off-screen fights. All my possessions fit into a small cardboard box: a single mug shaped like a pyramid and a mousepad styled like a miniature Arabian carpet. I avoid eye contact with the others and head for the lifts.

I wanted to be Truman Capote researching leads in that Kansas farmhouse, Woodward and Bernstein getting a scoop in a parking lot, Christiane Amanpour interviewing a war criminal on CNN. Instead, here I am being fired from a shitty tabloid website, deep-throating my own disgrace. A couple of years ago, I was questioning the Egyptian Minister of Youth about human rights like an intrepid AAP reporter. How has it come to this?

'Is that the ISIS flag?' Barclay shouted during my tour of the office a week earlier. The Shahada was written in white letters on black fabric, murkily visible through a window and broadcast on the TV in the staff kitchen.

'You can read Arabic, right?' he blurted, more a command than a question.

Daily News readers consume terrorism articles like hungry street dogs eat trash. There's not much nutritional value in these stories, it's the paint by numbers: 'He was always religious' or 'He took to fundamentalist ideology after his second divorce' kind of thing. These sensationalist smear stories play to the *Daily News*'s competitive advantage of running vulgar articles with colourful headlines like, 'My Father Was a Brutal, Amoral Sexual Predator Who Hated Women: Now He Goes By "Claire"'. Gawky-eyed UTS media graduates or desperate Sydney Uni journalists came to the *Daily News* to cut their teeth. This was the only company to accept my résumé after two years of applications and several unpaid internships, like a six-month stint at the *Inner West Courier*. All this had only resulted in a few by-lines, including my groundbreaking exposé about local pensioners who sewed winter sweaters for street dogs in Indonesia.

Barclay cut the tour short, saying that with my special knowledge of Arab culture, I should write a story about the unfolding terrorist attack at a chocolate cafe in Sydney's CBD, just a few hundred meters from where we were. The air was thick with panic, the city's pulse suddenly disrupted, as lives were torn apart in a place that should have been safe. I set to work immediately, nestling into a desk in a dark corner to devotedly craft the important journalistic details and ignoring the *click-clack* of the staff writers.

I began a rolling chronological account: 9.44am, the gunman is spotted through the cafe window with a ponytail that reaches to his waist and one long fingernail; 3.37 pm, some of the victims escape the cafe; 4.15pm, police are seen milling around, their tight uniforms showing their broad muscles, their faces fraught with worry.

I relished the chance to put my major in Arabic and Islamic studies to use for the first time ever, inserting a cunning assessment of the rise of the Islamic State in Syria and Iraq.

When Barclay read it half an hour later, he growled, 'Why didn't you put a picture of the ISIS flag right at the top?'

He elected to run the headline, 'Terrorist Brandishes ISIS Propaganda' and cut most of the historical context. It doesn't matter, I told myself. I was in the fast-paced world of news now and Barclay was the top dog.

It was with similar reverence that I treated Arthur Mansfield, a veteran journalist in his fifties, who was overseeing the training of all new hires for our second day in the office. Gruff, calloused by British tabloid culture and slightly hunched from too many long-haul flights between *Daily News* offices across the globe: Arthur was old-school print journalism personified, vulgar and to the point.

'Right, first one to identify all the typos in these stories gets their name on the board.'

We pored over dozens of stories in meeting room 6, which was called 'Eora'. The stories ranged in scope and tone from 'Crocodile Eats Man: Wife Says It Was Only a Matter of Time!'

to the loftier 'Supreme Court Judge Found in Bed With Mistress During Recess'.

'They say journalism is dying, but let me tell you, this is the best bloody job in the world!' Arthur croaked. 'Short of actually being an actor, this is play-acting: you get to explore whatever stories you want, follow in the footsteps of any career you like, be anyone you like ... Now, here are three headlines. I'll buy a Guinness for the first of you to tell me which uses the Oxford comma correctly.'

I had been taught that journalism was the bastion of democracy, the fourth estate, keeping the courts and government in check. Instead, this website was concerned with the social perils of public housing and the latest conspiracy about Princess Diana's death. Across the meeting room, I made eye contact with Mabinty, a Nigerian-American girl, who was smirking at the stupidity of the task. She seemed to get it.

Over drinks at the courtyard bar of the building housing the *Daily News* offices, which had been opened by Prince Charles when he visited Australia in the 70s, Mabinty and I sipped G&Ts and dissected the trashiness of the gig.

'Well, my dad is a Pentecostal preacher, and in America I would host evangelical TV shows and YouTube interviews with pastors TD Jakes and Creflo Dollar. So I get that sometimes you need a bit of flash to get a message across.' Mabinty sipped her drink carefully, her straightened hair falling delicately around her ears, which were studded with sleepers and white-gold gems. Her lips were glossily pink and her teeth brilliant white.

'I guess it just wasn't what I was expecting, you know?' I

confessed. 'I'm a person of faith too, but this is not what I had in mind when I asked Jesus to give me a job in journalism.' I stared down at my drink, then up at *The Project* on Channel 10, where Egyptian-Australian host Waleed Aly was decrying the Islamic State, saying, 'Terrorism is a grotesque form of theatre.'

'Babe,' Mabinty offered, grabbing my hand comfortingly, 'this is just a gig. It's a stepping stone – do what you have to do and move on.'

I nodded, throwing back my drink in one gulp. She smiled approvingly, the brightness of her teeth hurting my eyes.

~

'Mate, you have to think about our readership,' Barclay began on day three in the office. 'Honestly, people just don't care about social justice or the Arab Spring: they want the news, quick and easy. Grocery prices, *Big Brother* winners, Muslim immigration, that kind of thing.'

I nodded, getting the point but disappointed that none of my pitches had piqued his interest.

'Rewrite this for me ASAP', I saw in my inbox at my desk later: Barclay had sent me a story. I set to work immediately, laying out the story of a group of refugees who had arrived on a rickety boat from Indonesia and then been sent back because of Operation Sovereign Borders. I mention that they were forced to leave all their belongings save for what they could carry and that several women were pregnant. It was a humanitarian disaster right on our doorstep – I was sure I had met his brief. Within minutes, the story was up, but the headline wasn't quite what I expected: 'Refugees Come With Their Bags Packed, Determined to Move into Our Neighbourhoods'.

Out of the corner of my eye, I saw a woman in the graphic design section slowly pixelating the nipple of one of the twin sisters from *Big Brother*. The nipple had been magnified to an enormous size, filling up the entire screen of her iMac, staring out, vast and terrible like the Eye of Sauron. There was rage in my belly and self-pity in my heart. I threw down my pen and went home for the day.

'How was work, ya big journalist enta?' Mum asked, shelling fuul into a bowl and watching video clips on Aghapy TV of scenes from *The Passion of the Christ* set to the voiceover of Pope Shenouda reading Psalm 23. 'Did you write some very important stuff?'

'Yeah, Mum, it was great, very busy, lots of big stories about the news, politics.' I refrained from telling her that I had compiled a listicle of famous celebrity dogs.

'Yalla, habibi, we proud of you! Dinner ready soon.'

I shut the door and threw myself onto my bed facedown, falling asleep to the sound of Christ's agonised shrieks.

The next day, all of the trainee journos, including Mabinty and me, got called to the editorial desk for our daily briefing: there had been a spate of stories with shonky spelling, including an article that had gone live with the headline, 'Think of a Headline Here'.

Greg, the editor-in-chief, let the journo go and was set to grill the rest of us. 'No typos! No typos! I want maximum efficiency, more stories … but no typos! Well, what are you all standing around for looking like sewer rats? Get to work!'

We rushed back to our desks.

In my harried state, it occurred to me that I had nothing to report on. Or rather, nothing worth the Walkley Award that I had envisioned myself winning, with Waleed Aly handing it to me in my waking dream, saying, 'I'm proud of you, habibi,' and kissing me once on each cheek, hand lingering over my shoulder.

I snapped to it: the options were sparse. I could write about Nigella Lawson 'looking svelte in a sheer black dress with her brunette locks flowing down', but decided it was not really my lane. Maybe a piece about the dangers of farmed Tasmanian Atlantic salmon. Or perhaps something about the housing crisis – oh, yes, that shouted 'investigative journalist'.

That was when it hit me. At a local suburban newspaper I had interned for last year, I created a profile for a woman named Sung-Lee, a Chinese exchange student, and asked local renters on Gumtree and Facebook Marketplace if they could give me free accommodation in exchange for 'other services'. It was a risky move reusing the story, potentially infringing the newspaper's copyright claims to the article. Benedict, the editor, a staunch Roman Catholic who I had met at mass at Sydney Uni's Catholic Society chapel – who once tried to sue Channel 9 for covering the Gay and Lesbian Mardi Gras, saying, 'Sodom doesn't deserve the promo' – had run my piece next to an ad for a Catholic retirement home.

With Barclay's words ringing in my ear, his demand for 'a new story, something hot and compelling, ASAP', and having come up empty after pondering for two hours, I pushed aside the fear and the sense of risk. I decided to 'repurpose' the story with some tweaking for the *Daily News*. I was finished within an hour, screenshots and captions in place, headline virtually jumping off the page: 'Sex for Rent: Australian Men Using Gumtree and Facebook to Make Sleazy Offers of Free Accommodation by Asking Vulnerable Women "What Favours Would You Provide?"' But then I was hit with a pang of doubt: Benedict's shrew-like face flashed into my mind's eye. My face felt hot and hands clammy, and the air in the room was stale and smelled of mould. I needed to go for a walk.

'Lord, what would you have me do?' I asked myself. 'Give me a sign, any sign, to know that if I do this I'll still have your favour.' I looked to the crucifix at St Michael's, down the street from the office. I saw the stations of the cross all around me and wondered how the *Daily News* would cover the *Passion* story: 'Local Carpenter Commits Treason, Declares Himself King of the Jews, Friends Say, "I Don't Know Him"'.

A message buzzing in my pocket woke me like a cock's crow. It was from Barclay: 'Where r u? Story needs to go up within half hour, not meeting quota!'

Back in our building, the lifts opened to reveal Mabinty's gleaming white teeth.

'Hey, babe, you okay? You look worried. Give it to Jesus, hunny. We're too blessed to be stressed.'

I said, 'Amen, sister,' but couldn't bring myself to look at her in the eyes.

On the way to my desk, I spotted Arthur Mansfield in the cafeteria. I told him I had written a story for another paper once and wanted to reuse it now. His answer was concise: 'You've got to decide: is your career important to you?' Then he removed a pickle from a jar with his bare fingers and shoved it into his mouth. 'You have to make that choice,' he said, munching, spraying out a fine mist of vinegar.

Give it to Jesus, hunny.

Yalla, habibi, we proud of you!

Is your career important to you?

Back at my desk, my head swirled with these competing phrases. To run the story or archive it, that was the question. I glanced up at the editors' section and saw Barclay cock his head around his computer, glaring at me and tapping his watch. Hurry up, his gesture said.

I clicked 'publish'.

How to Win a Case

Bribe the judge and justice will prevail.

The chambers are faux mahogany. The chords of Beethoven's *Symphony No. 5* thrum dramatically: *da da da dum*. 'Daniel is an unmarried twenty-seven-year-old and his mother's only son,' a voice announces in baritone. A lamp descends from the ceiling, illuminating the chambers of Judge Judith Sheindlin, who goes by Judge Judy for TV purposes.

I've always been a little scared and impressed by this clear-eyed bastion of justice. I watched her every afternoon in 2007 from 4.30pm to 5pm, but now she appears before me in the flesh to govern my choices and decide my fate.

'Samira is a fifty-eight-year-old Egyptian woman. Her son says that she doesn't support his dreams. She says that he needs to get his act together, get his head out of the clouds and give her grandchildren.'

I have no defence lawyer, I have to stage and win my own suit against Mum and the audience is composed of little old church ladies dressed in black.

I look sideways. Byrd the bailiff stares back shrewdly. His posture is firm and rigid and his shirt is wrapped tight around his low-hanging paunch. Does he ever get to use his gun? I wonder. And why does he look so much like my uncle Kareem? Now that I look closer, I see that Byrd has Kareem's receding hairline, hook nose and thick, bushy eyebrows. His Medicare card appears where his name tag should be, which says 'Kareem Youssef'.

'What are some of the infringements or violations you'd like to bring against your son, Mrs Nour?' Judge Judy asks in her nasal tone.

'When is he going to get it together and give us grandchildren? Lazem yeshoof 7alo!' Mum answers in a high-pitched plea. There is a ripple of muttering through the sea of church ladies, and one of them says, 'He wasn't even watching his grandad when he died.' The others suck their teeth and shake their heads.

'Will the audience please be quiet!' Judge Judy shouts. 'Mrs Nour, I don't speak Arabic,' she says, turning sharply on Mum.

'But you are Arab, no?'

'I'm an Ashkenazi Jew.'

'Ah, then you should understand! Where are the grandkids?' Mum continues. 'He is not talking to anyone. What are his friends going to do for him? Friends get you nowhere! You understand this, sister?'

Dad is sitting in the witness stand.

'Sir, do you have anything to add?' Judge Judy asks, looking like a hawk with her billowy black cape and sharp features.

'I always say, "Any girls in your group of friends?" and he always says, "No, no".'

The church ladies mutter and one of them grunts, 'Astaghfirullah Al Azeem.'

Mum and Dad's other critiques include the way I dress strangely with 'jeans that have tears in them', that my friends are 'faffy boys' all working in the arts, and that I don't go with them to church anymore. 'He doesn't remember the Lord!' Dad shouts, garnering a look of judgement from Judge Judith Sheindlin.

'Be quiet, sir. Why are you speaking? Did I ask you to speak? Quiet.'

Dad's mouth droops like mine did when he would tell me off for not cleaning my room during all those years of childhood.

'Well, it seems to me that this is an open-and-shut case,' Judge Judy continues. 'Your parents wanted your help and support, but you're an artistic slacker' – she draws out the word 'slacker', getting a low chuckle from Bailiff Kareem and a round of laughs from the audience – 'who couldn't give them what they deserved.'

'Aren't you supposed to be hear me out? You seem pretty one-sided and biased for a judge!' I tell her, frustration making my eyes water and filling my chest with heat.

'That's baloney, sir! Baloney! You owe your mother two grandchildren, a nice wife and a career in the law.'

The old ladies break into applause. 'That's how it should be,' I hear them mutter in Arabic.

I scream as the bailiff takes me by the arm and leads me to the dock. It's dark and there is no air here. The walls shrink around me like the Chokey from *Matilda*.

'I can't pay! I can't pay!' I yell into the void as I'm dragged into the dark. 'I can't pay ...'

How to Date Women

Better your uncle's daughter than a stranger's: the devil you know brings no surprises.

Another Bayside Christian community youth group, another opportunity to hear about marriage and the virtue of saving yourself until the wedding night.

Everyone is making googly eyes at each other, and a group of eighteen-year-old guys leer over at a bevvy of girls with keratin-straightened hair, who pretend not to notice while pouting at the altar. The smell of the barbecue, which one of the uncles always works when it's not Lent or Advent, wafts from the courtyard all the way down the aisles and into the sanctuary. The hotplate sizzles with fat from plump kofta, smoky chicken wings and umami-rich beef patties topped with sweet caramelised onion.

'Brothers, God loves for a man to have sex with his wife. Imagine waking up one morning to the fresh face and beautiful body of that special girl. As she opens her legs to you, so does

Christ open his heart for the Church,' Father Constantinos proclaims.

Before church, I had just finished an episode of *Nigella Kitchen*, my favourite thing to do when stressed. I'm unemployed again, tutoring HSC English for $20 an hour at a dingy Bankstown 'pre-university college' all weekend: sex before marriage really hasn't presented itself as a temptation.

All around me, hormones are raging. After mass, girlfriends and boyfriends as young as fifteen will pair up to hold each other's hands and, for the daring, escape to the storage room to go to second base and really let the Spirit take over. I have nobody and feel more out of place than ever, especially after what Father Constantinos told me last week.

'Brother, you've got to find yourself a wife,' he said during confession. 'Honestly, you're in that perfect age frame and I could connect you with so many lovely Coptic girls.'

I looked up at a picture of Saint Euphrosynos the Cook, who was known for having received a taste of the holy apples of paradise, fresh and crisp and probably not sour like Granny Smiths can be. I told Father Constantinos that I could handle this myself and promised to give it a go.

For two years now, I've been teaching Sunday school with a girl called Jennifer Eskander, who is actually my second cousin on Dad's side. With her long, skinny legs and big head with its slightly jutting chin and broad forehead, she looks like a shoebill stork.

I've never really thought of her in *that* way before, but we do text a lot, mostly about lesson plans. Now and again, she sends me photos of the boxes of near-spoiled bananas her dad buys at Paddy's Markets. In turn, I send her recordings of scenes of Egyptian mosalsalats – one of Hajj Metwalee's wives serves him a whole plate of stuffed pigeons and he shouts, 'Mish keda ya waleeyah! Not like this, woman!'

I decide to man up. I decide to play the field. I decide to 'talk' to Jennifer.

Looking down at my phone from the back pew, I Facebook message her: 'I think u look nice.' She is wearing a pink Nike hoodie and her hair is up in a knot. She says nothing for a while. I wait for the ellipsis that signals a response. Then ...

'So do u.'

A few weeks later, I'm eating a fuul sandwich with the boys after liturgy and Jennifer looks at me from across the youth hall like I am a fat, bubbling pork chop.

'You're in, bro! You're definitely in now!' my stupid cousins Shoukry and Ayman jeer, spraying stray bits of fava bean onto the concrete.

In that night's youth group meeting, Father Constantinos is saying something about how Adam was made to pay for the sin of lusty Eve. From my corner seat in the back pew, I'm scrolling my 'men's fitness and training' Pinterest board. Muscular athletes, gleaming in baby-oiled contrapposto, lift my soul to God. Out of the corner of my eye, I see Jennifer pull out her phone, so I check Facebook to see if she's messaging. Three dots appear beneath her name.

…

'We'd really like to have you over next Saturday night.'

…

'Sure, that sounds nice! Should I bring anything?'

…

'Just bring yourself 😉'

~

On Saturday, I pull up to the Eskander house in Liverpool. All the stone lions have been frontlit, giving a majestic air, and the water fountain around the statue of the Virgin Mary is flowing loudly. Jennifer greets me at the door in a figure-hugging black sleeveless dress that I've never seen on my Pinterest. She apologises for the house not being very clean, though all the surfaces are shiny.

The family are all in the living room. Mr Eskander looks thin at first, but then I notice the belly that sticks out low and round, hanging above the tight waist of his suit pants, which cover skinny legs. He shakes my hand. Jennifer's brother, Fady, gets up off the couch when he sees me. He is in clean Adidas tracksuit pants and white, new-looking TNs. Tant Mona is in a velvety purple dress that makes her look like an old bridesmaid.

In the dining room, there is a richly laden banquet-style table, and I sit down to a meal of molokheya and chicken, which is said to give newlyweds special erotic powers.

'Habibi, e7na ma bena3rafsh na3zem,' Tant Mona tells me,

placing an oven-baked Maryland chicken leg onto my plate, upon which she pours a ladleful of viscous green molokheya. 'We don't stand on ceremony here.'

We start eating. Icons of giant saints hang all around the room, including one of Saint George, who is about to impale a trapped lizard with a giant spear.

'Have you heard you can torrent the original Tomb Raider games on PC?' I say to Fady, thinking he looks good with his fresh fade.

Mr Eskander clears his throat loudly at the end of the table. 'My daughter is interested in you,' he says. 'Now that you have expressed your interest, we expect that you will make your intentions clear. Are you able to support her? How much does your job pay?'

I look at Jennifer. She rolls her eyes but smiles at me. I turn to Fady, who winks. The mother stares back at me expectantly over the dead bird.

Suddenly my face is tingly and I feel sick. I rise abruptly, the heavy wooden chair sliding against the sparkly white tiles. I cropdust my way to the door, lying that my dad has just texted me to get to church for Gidoo's annual memorial service, leaving a cloud of translucent gas in my wake.

I can hear Mr Eskander berating his daughter inside after he slams the door shut behind me. 'How could you be interested in a donkey like this, ya bent el habla?' Jennifer looks at me with sad eyes through the window.

Driving down the M5 from Liverpool to Bankstown, my

heart is racing, my chest is pounding. I play a podcast with Nigella Lawson talking about her favourite Christmas dishes to unwind.

'Did you hear that Danny is trying it on with Jennifer Eskander?' All the Sunday school students are talking about it after mass the following week. That's when Jennifer walks through the crowd, turning her head over her shoulder to see if she can find me. Not wanting to be entrapped in an awkward conversation, I hide in the church cafeteria near the salt bags, eating a white roll with scrambled eggs in silence.

At our next confession, Father Constantinos gets all serious with me. He doesn't even start with one of his lame Bible jokes, such as after confession last week when he asked, 'Who was the greatest comedian in the Bible?' Then, breaking into a smile, he answered, 'Samson. He brought the house down,' and slapped my knee by way of a punchline.

'Danny, I sense you are struggling.'

A pleading tone escapes me. 'Not at all, Father, I am as strong in the Lord as ever.'

Father picks the lint from the elbow patches of his robe before continuing, his long nose elongating in judgement. 'Jennifer feels that you wouldn't be "up to the job", so to speak, in the marital duties department.'

With big eyes and mouth agape, I shake my head. I should be offended but only feel relief, a sudden loosening of tension in the knots around my neck.

'Habibi,' he says, 'you're getting old.' It is two weeks until my twenty-eighth birthday. 'It's time to get serious. You need to think about your future.'

When I get home that afternoon, I join Mum and Dad on the couch where they're watching liturgy on Holy Cross TV, an Egyptian channel that always shows footage of the patriarch healing the infirm and the lame.

'Woman was placed in man's path as a temptation, but can he overcome? Can he work with her as a partner?' says the Holy Father to a silent and reverent crowd.

Mum asks me if I'm still 'talking to' Jennifer, especially after her father called to tell Dad off for raising such an indecisive son.

'I'm talking to everyone, Mum,' I say.

On the TV, the patriarch throws a handful of salt at an icon of a saint and the crowd breaks into applause.

'You need to get yourself a woman,' Dad says, spitting pumpkin seed shells into a small bowl.

Scrolling Insta, I see that Nigella Lawson has posted her salted chocolate tart recipe. Digging further, I find out that she's coming to Sydney to give a talk on 'why food matters'. I always thought that food mattered because we need it to survive, but Nigella will say something much more profound. I message Jennifer, deciding to give it 'another go'.

'Want to see Nigella?'

'Yeah sure, love her so much!'

'Yep, she's gorgeous, good on Palestine too,' I respond, remembering when she posted about the origins of hummus.

On the feast day of Saint Sebastian, who was shot through

with Roman arrows while strapped naked to a pole, I anxiously await Nigella's arrival on stage. A stillness falls across the crowd, the kind of suspenseful excitement that comes before a good meal.

In walks Nigella, in a chic black pantsuit, slender of form and loping of gait. Her hair is long and dark. Her skin is like macadamia-nut milk, which is expensive and better for the rainforests than soy. She speaks like she has a plum or a Jerusalem fig in her mouth. If Nancy Ajram is a sparkling champagne, then Nigella is a fine, rich merlot.

An hour later and after she says something about how cooking her dead mum's chicken feels like a prayer of devotion, it's time for audience questions. I walk to the aisle where a microphone stand has been set up, my nerves jangling and frenzied. Out of the corner of my eye I see Jennifer nodding her assent, a little smile at the corner of her mouth. Maybe my boldness pleases her.

I've been thinking on this question all afternoon. I know Jennifer will like it. 'How clever you are to have thought of something so outside the box,' she will say later tonight at Cairo Summer cafe.

'Nigella, you often talk about the pleasure of food, but what do you do on those days when you're too stressed to eat?' If the mic was handheld, I would drop it now.

She ponders seriously, looking pale and wondrous as the moon. 'Don't force it. Have you tried soup?'

Wow, what a thing to say, I think, thanking her and returning to my seat.

Later at Cairo Summer, Jennifer and I have the falafel and talk about our parents' migration stories. 'My aunty came on a boat,' she says, munching fluorescent pink turnip pickles. Then they bring out the main course: samak 7arra2, baked fish in a red sauce. I eat too quickly, sauce smearing my chin.

'Wow, you must really like fish,' Jennifer says, crossing her fine legs under the counter.

I say, 'Actually, I've never been much of a fish eater.'

That's when we're joined by an Asian girlfriend of Jennifer's, whose name is Hannah Om. I sometimes see Hannah at mass, but I'm confused about why she's suddenly on our date.

Hannah, whose dad is gyppo, is also half-Filipino. I've always called Filos the Egyptians of Asia, because they're fun and goofy and know how to have a good time.

'I hope you don't mind but Hannah was in the area so I texted her.'

'No, I don't mind at all,' I say, swallowing my confusion and rage, itchy and hot around my temples.

Hannah spends the whole night telling us about her gluten intolerance. When I get to Bankstown Station, I find that my car has been keyed along its side in cruel, jagged streaks. I drive home fuming.

'How was the date?' Mum and Dad ask, but I ignore them, walking upstairs to my room and slamming the door.

I call Jennifer. 'I thought we were on a date tonight?'

A long pause. I wonder if she's heard me and am about to ask again before she breaks the silence.

'What … what … gave you that idea?'

'We both love Nigella. You liked the question I asked her. I caught you smiling at me.'

There is further silence on the other side of the line. 'Hmmm … I think you might have the wrong idea about us,' Jennifer responds. 'I feel like you don't really know what you want, to be honest.'

I tell her I'll see her at Sunday school, then turn on my laptop and watch an episode of *Nigella Feasts*.

'Even if you don't have the most expensive ingredients, you can still make a really delicious meal,' Nigella says, stirring pureed pumpkin into cream and vegetable stock.

I go downstairs to make myself a kebda sandwich with chilli sauce and eat it in my underwear on my bed. I wake up with a stomach-ache.

How to Become a Father

Come to me, all you who are weary and heavy-laden,
and I will give you jest!

At Our Lady of the Holy Cross boys' October getaway, Father Constantinos tells the youth leaders that 'anyone who gives even a cup of cold water to one of these little ones as a disciple will gain their reward..'

After praying the Angelus, we leave the chapel for a match of tag football: leaders versus kids. 'Run, you stupid donkeys, don't just stand there!' Father Constantinos shouts at a group of twelve-year-olds, throwing cold water all over his 'suffer the little children' sentiment moments earlier.

Lunch at the Monastery of the Good Shepherd Youth Centre is a stringy chicken breast, a clumpy mound of mashed potato and a greyish sauce pooling around a scattering of mushy baby peas like sheep without a shepherd.

Father pulls up a chair next to me. 'Danny, I've been thinking,' he begins, rustling the folds of his gown like Professor Snape. 'You should become a priest.'

Apart from the need for more 'young men of God' in our community, he also mentions my series of failed dates with girls, including my second cousin Jennifer. 'I mean, that was really bad, habibi. Her dad wanted me to remove you from the parish,' he says while working on a mouthful of the potato mash. Before he goes, he hands me a booklet that says '10 Steps for Discerning and Deciding', which has a photo of the archbishop smiling with a group of postulants in their early twenties, so younger than me.

I need to take stock, to figure out if this is what I really want to do or if I'm just following the community script. First, I speak to the young trainee priest they've rostered for this camp. He's a tall, milk-fed golden retriever of a man whose name is Corbin Mcaughan and who is the eldest of seven. He stands upright, chest broad and smile beaming. His hair is blond, shiny and lustrous. He'd be a great poster child for the Third Reich if his family wasn't completely Irish on both sides.

'It was always my mum's dream for me to become a priest, and I'm just pumped to be doing the Father's bidding. Did I want to have a family? Of course! That would have been lovely! But my life on this path is so rich and full of blessings that, honestly, I have no regrets,' he says in one breathy huff, catching and throwing a football back and forth with a group of Year 6 kids.

Then there's Joseph Sammoun. I've always felt nervous around Joseph. He's not charming, or even good-looking, but he has this weirdly intense presence: you can feel him staring at you even after you've looked away. He's a postulant, which means he's still 'discerning' the priesthood.

'Do it only if you really want, man – that's what I'd say. It's a hard life otherwise,' he tells me, midway through writing a sermon in his austere, prison-like bedroom.

I see the top of his page, which says, 'Why celibacy is a gift', and leave him to it, seeing his sad eyes long after I've stepped away.

I call Mum to get a third opinion. It's 4pm on a Sunday, so I know she will be sitting at her vanity applying a thick layer of Nivea from a blue metallic container, as she always does after church lunch at Our Lady of the Holy Cross.

'Mama, 3yz aba2a a2sis, eh ra2yik?' I say. 'Mum, I want to be a priest. What do you think?'

'Eh? A2sis? No, that's just because you're around Catholics.'

I can almost see her face scrunched up with consternation.

'Why you don't want to give me grandchildren, habibi? Marriage is a blessing also,' she says, her voice now pleading and squeaky. 'The priests, you know they cannot have children,' she adds, believing this will dissuade me when it's actually an important part of my whole motivation.

'But Mum, isn't it an honour for a mother to give her child to God?' I ask her briskly.

'You will bring my head down into the dirt with shame,' she responds curtly in Arabic, hanging up on me.

After this pep talk, I run into Father Constantinos.

'Father, I'm not sure if it's for me,' I say, my stomach having soured with hours of anxious indecision.

He says, 'Habibi, I want you to use the next few days as a kind of spiritual retreat: pretend like you're in the priesthood. Eat prayerfully, walk prayerfully, pray the liturgy of the hours.' He tells me God will show me the path.

For the rest of the afternoon break, with the kids down at the pool or playing basketball, I walk around the campsite, taking in the cafeteria, the photos of all the abbots, the cold serenity of the chapel, a tragic pietà and the red flame hanging aloft in the lantern showing that the holy presence is in the sanctuary.

A loneliness washes over me. Is this to be my life? A life safe from the obligations to marry and have kids, but of total and desolating aloneness? I've spent too long strolling. I'm late for Adoration. I tell one of the kids off for shouting in the corridor outside of chapel and run inside. I sit next to Joseph.

Father Corbin is lecturing us on the sin of Adam, his voice droning over the hum of the ceiling fan. He spends way too long describing how Eve seduced Adam, mopping his brow with a handkerchief even though the chapel is air-conditioned.

My knee brushes Joseph's. Neither of us moves. My skin prickles as if the weight of inherited sin has settled in this one accidental touch. For the rest of the service, as I try to focus on the Latin in the hymnal, Joseph's presence looms like a shadow over my shoulder. He's clutching his rosary, the beads slipping through his fingers. I give him intense side eye, watching the soft formation of 'Hail Mary' on his hairy lips. Those lips pull me in like Moses to the burning bush.

Then it's time for the youth leaders to get ready for mass. Alone with him in the vestibule, I adjust Joseph's collar. My fingers linger, brushing the fabric. There's an electric hum between us, a frisson that spreads like static through my chest. He smells of fresh grass and earth, and the scent anchors itself in my brain like a rainbow, like God's promise after the flood where he killed everyone in a bout of rage. Maybe Yahweh was hangry that day, I think, snapping back to myself.

Mass feels endless. Now it's Father Constantinos' turn to berate us, and he does so with the story of Saint Valentine, who was beaten with clubs and then beheaded outside the Flaminian Gate. I'm distracted by the vibration in my pocket. I check my phone – an email from the *Inner West Courier*.

'We have an opening for a temporary contract. Would you like to start Tuesday?' the message reads.

My chest expands with hope and panic. Is this the answer to my prayers?

At dinner, the children are seated in rows, their chatter filling the dining hall like birdsong. We ladle food onto their plates – spaghetti and meatballs tonight, with rolls and butter for sides. 'Say your grace,' Joseph reminds a group of boys, his voice low but firm. I catch a glimpse of his profile as he leans down to help a younger kid with their napkin and a pang of something sharp twists inside me.

Later, the children have questions, always questions. 'Why do we have to pray so much?' one boy asks. I stumble through an answer about the importance of being close to God, but my own words feel hollow. Joseph steps in smoothly, offering an analogy: prayer is like sunlight for a growing tree. The boy nods, satisfied, and Joseph smiles. I only see his sad, lonesome eyes.

Then more sport; this time, soccer. Leaders versus kids. My heart races, not with excitement but with dread. I've always hated sport. In Year 2, I prayed for a T-ball game to be cancelled and when the rain came, I believed in God's love for the first time. I pull on one of our church jerseys, which say 'Holy Cross', with a picture of an angel holding a football: meant to be fun.

As the game begins, I collide with Joseph. Our shoulders brush and his woody, sweaty funk hits me like a wave. His bedraggled hair clings to his forehead and he looks wild, like a sewer rat after a flood. A tingling nervousness creeps down my spine, then lower. My breath catches in my throat.

Back at the house, the children are finally asleep and the camp quiets. Through the paper-thin wall, I hear Joseph reciting the Litany of the Sacred Heart with a fervour that suggests he's repenting for something specific. I sit on my bed, staring at the screen of my phone, wondering if he knows I can hear him.

I scroll through my phone in an absent-minded moment of horny desperation. I go to one of my old faithfuls, an app called Scruff, for men who like men. Hairy men. Short Arabs, tall Greeks and a guy called 'Hung_habibi_lover_69'. That's when I see Joseph, sprawled naked on a couch, his manhood on display for God, the cherubim and all the saints. The thought slices through me like a knife. As a dog returns to its vomit, I think bitterly. But the bitterness twists into something else as I imagine his sad eyes, his gaunt face and the pale, thin legs that jut out of his basketball shorts. My neck grows hot and my hand slips beneath the waistband of my Kmart undies. I descend into a few moments of pleasure, a slow and steady jerking escalating into frenzied madness.

The aftermath is a spiral. Relief comes first, but shame follows quickly, pooling over me like sulphur over Gomorrah. I lie awake that night, haunted by visions of fire and brimstone, imagining the gates of hell waiting to swallow me whole.

By morning, I've made my decision. I hastily throw my clothes into a bag, my hands trembling. Driving down the seminary's wooded driveway feels like an escape from something monstrous – or perhaps a surrender.

I swing past a Kmart to buy new collared shirts for Tuesday morning, trying not to think about the grassy smell of Joseph's collar or the desperate look in his eyes. That weekend, as I pore over the *Inner West Courier*'s style manual, I absently toss the kids camp prayer book into the bin. The pages flutter, settling among the garbage.

Father Constantinos texts me. 'U should have stayed.'

I stare at the bin, then back at my phone. I shove it in the drawer and slam it shut. Forgive me, Father.

How to Get Married

Where goes the ugly woman, so follows the fat daughter.

Wog weddings drive me nuts. Ascending the garish imitation-marble tiled staircase, gleaming white beneath the glare of the 9000 fluorescent halogen globes, I am usually greeted with giant words emblazoned in electric bulbs: 'El Paradiso' or 'La Renaissance' or 'Imperial Regency', or any other weird abstraction of a phrase from one of the Romance languages. Tonight, it's the Imperial Regency.

Then, reaching the summit of the steps, I am greeted with the guest list, which sits on a stand and is encased in a giant photo frame with a golden border. Here are some of the names:

Noor El-Noor
Nour El-Noor
Noureen El-Noor
Nourhane El-Noor

Nourhanne El-Noor
Noor Noor
Noreen Noor
Nourhane Noor
Noor Nour
Norhane Nour
Noureen Nour

Just as I am feeling overwhelmed, I find my name. That's when I notice the middle-aged couple to my right. They look confused; the man has his arms crossed and the woman is shaking her head furiously. After checking, they discover that their names aren't on the guest list.

'How could they do this to us?' the woman asks in Arabic.

'I told you that family have always been trash,' the man responds.

I suspect this may have something to do with them having never returned their RSVPs.

The father of the bride walks out with his arms wide open. The couple stop muttering. 'Ahlan w sahlan ya a7la naas,' he says, which roughly translates to, 'A thousand welcomes to the very best of people.' I feel relieved and walk quickly inside.

There are more imitation-marble tiles in the reception centre and even more halogen globes hanging high above the dance floor. There are also three giant glass(ish) chandeliers surrounded by a halo of (fake) white lilies. There are dozens of rows of tables:

some are right at the edge of the room, and the people on them look tiny from where I am standing.

I bump into Aunty Aida, who says, 'Look how skinny you're getting,' which is a disguised jab at my mother's cooking. Aunty Aida has hated my mother ever since she 'stole' her fiancé in the 70s, who is now my father.

At the head of the space is a long Last Supper–style table where the bride and the groom are to sit, alongside their parents, friends and siblings. In many ways, this *is* their Last Supper: it is the last time they will be together without the burden of children; it is the last time they will smile and laugh with their in-laws; it is the last time the couple will be truly happy.

When I arrive at my table, a group of men and women in their mid-thirties look over at me. The men are swarthy, their hair slicked back with gel and shirts open down to the navel, revealing thick black tufts of hair. They also have very thick moustaches, which are not being grown for Movember or even ironically. The girls are dressed in stretchy, figure-hugging polyester-blend dresses, which accentuate their busts and cover the entire length of their arms, hooking over their thumbs with thin fabric loops. They wear a lot of eye makeup and, along with the men, make a lot of direct eye contact.

Their gaudy self-adornment and unashamed, almost predatory staring tell me that these people are 'fresh off the boat'. Their manners are as raw as the minced lamb being served on small plates along the length of the table.

'Are you from here or from there?' one of the men asks me.

'No, I am from here,' I respond.

'Yes, you act like you are from here, but you look like you are from there.'

I concentrate on the food to distract myself from this unfortunate exchange. The table is long and richly laid, and the food is decadent, reminiscent of a bacchanalian Roman orgy. It includes:

hundreds of pink slivers of flaccid pickled turnip
many small plates of strong, sharp feta covered in black nigella seeds
mounds of vine leaves, chunky and gleaming with a sticky white film
shankleesh: a dry, mouldy cheese, sour-smelling and mixed with parsley and tomatoes
creamy plates of baba ghanoush and hummus, both blushing red with paprika
hard shards of flatbread, fried, golden and crunchy
luscious, thick round cuts of eggplant sitting in a small pool of garlicky oil
hot balls of falafel: brown on the outside and vibrant green within
assorted salted nuts: cashews, corn kernels, walnuts
almonds sitting in small bowls of icy water
tabouleh, verdant like a garden in spring

There's also alcohol: each table has a big round bottle of aged Chivas Regal whisky and a skinny long bottle of cold Belvedere Vodka.

Later, I am roused from my eating by the voice of the emcee. 'Ladieeees and gentlemen, boyyys and girlsss, it's time for this party to get starteddd ...' A baby is screaming incessantly at the far end of the reception centre. It is a high-pitched, shrieking wail, which makes me feel that someone should call an exorcist. 'Let's all take our seats and put our hands togetherrrr!' the emcee continues, in a tone that makes me expect a boxing match to begin.

'Please welcome the father and mother of the bride, Mr and Mrs El-Noooooooooor!'

Two French-style doors swing open and a small middle-aged woman enters, bopping up and down in a powder-blue pantsuit and elaborately drawn makeup, her hair in a high chignon. Her husband follows closely behind, wearing a navy-blue polyester suit and a white lily boutonniere on his lapel. He claps his hands intermittently and shakes his hips stiffly. Very loud New York hip-hop from the late 90s plays with lurid sexual expletives.

These same introductions are repeated thirty-five times for other family members, including an uncle who flew in from the Middle East especially for the occasion. The screaming baby has not stopped wailing. Finally, it is time for the entry of the bride and the groom. Everyone stands, the excitement now palpable. Even the baby is quiet.

'Ladies and gentlemen, boys and girls, put your hands

together and raise your glasses for Mr and Mrs Nour El-Noor-Nour and Nourhane El-Noor-Nour!'

Mary J Blige's 'Family Affair' comes blaring out of the speaker and the doors swing open. Out streams a long procession of very muscular drummers in tight-fitting beige chinos, beating very big drums. The bride holds her bouquet up while she swings her hips, which are pulled in tight by a corset of satin lace. The groom's hands wave from left to right, his hair parted to one side, and he also shakes his hips energetically. Plumes of smoke cover their feet, erupting continuously from small trumpet-like machines on either side of the door.

Our clapping abates as the bridal party sits down. The main meal is served. It is option a or option b: a cut of lamb steak with steamed carrots, potato and mushroom sauce or a breast of chicken, also with steamed carrots, potato and mushroom sauce.

During the meal, I accidentally make eye contact with the foreigners at my table and turn away, embarrassed. One of the women keeps asking for something called a 'fruit cocktail'. 'Do you have fruit cocktail?' she asks three waiters, one after the other. They all shake their heads. She also seems confused. Eventually, one of the waiters just brings her an apple juice. The food is whisked away and the emcee announces, 'Let's hit the floor!' It is time to dance.

A throng floods the dance floor and carries the bride and groom off their feet. They are tossed up and down with abandon. The bride's veil falls off and floats to the ground, where it is trampled on by many feet, which move in a rhythmic, circular dabke. The group of strangers is looking at me again. I cannot avoid their gaze, so I go to dance with them.

I gyrate my hips in small circles with the group of five foreigners. Someone produces a fabric bracelet called a misbaha and flings it over and over again. I begin to sweat. Then I join the dance, which spins faster and faster until everyone becomes one giant blur. A teenage girl throws up onto the dance floor.

After the music quietens down, the floor empties so that the bride and groom can be photographed cutting the three-tier cake. Only the bottom layer is actual fruitcake, encased in a thick white marzipan icing; the two tiers on top are styrofoam.

Mariah Carey's 'Without You' plays through the speakers. In a sombre, soft voice, the emcee says, 'Let's welcome the beautiful couple to the dance floor once more, for their bridal waltz.'

During the bride and groom's slow, methodical dancing, the foreigners at my table pull their chairs close to mine. They tell me about their childhoods, their interests, the status of their visa applications. I begin to change my mind about these people: now the men seem charming and the women very chic.

It's time to watch the same-day video package, and all 490 guests stare up at the screen projection that now drops from the ceiling. We see the bride's makeup application at 5am this morning, we see the best man affixing the bow tie to the groom and, miraculously, the bridal waltz, which occurred merely minutes prior.

Now is when we must see the married couple off for their honeymoon. We form a long triangular prism from the bridal table all the way to the exit so that the couple can board their stretch Hummer and drive to the airport for their Carnival Cruise Line holiday to the French island territory of New Caledonia.

I hold hands with one of the foreigners and stare into her brown eyes as the newly married couple passes beneath our interlocked hands. It feels nice. I accept her marriage proposal. All the guests follow the couple out of the hall and I take my new wife home to meet my parents.

Now, we are married.

(Repeat ad infinitum.)

How to Have a Sick Parent

Your father wiped your shit when you were a child; now, you must clean him in his dotage.

When Dad has his heart attack, it is with a *galumph*, a falling and the reverberation shaking the upper level of our house.

Mum and I are watching *Titanic*, and as Jack and Rose are deep in the throes of lovemaking, a lusty hand raised to the steaming glass of a carriage window, we run upstairs to see Dad splayed out on the carpet: a mighty thing brought low.

He is out cold and his skin is clammy and cool. I can't really feel a heartbeat on his wrist but may be measuring it wrong because all I know about this practice has been learned from *Grey's Anatomy*. Rita is at work and can't offer any help. Dad doesn't respond to our shouts, nor to Mum spraying cologne into his face. Desperate for him to come to, I shout, 'Baba, there's a sale on mangoes: a box for five dollars!' which rouses him from his condition. He even responds, 'Get three boxes!'

We hear the ambulance siren out front and I run downstairs to let them in: a man and a woman. Dad is afraid of butch white ladies, so when one of the paramedics trudges up the stairs with her asymmetric haircut, broad shoulders and tattooed neck, I see his eyes widen with terror.

'So, what's happened today?' she asks.

'Oh, well, I've been very sick ... very, very sick,' Dad says. 'My back, my legs, my arms – everything hurts, everything bad.'

Kshhhk, says the walkie-talkie, and the woman walks back to the hallway to take the call with emergency services.

'She's a big one, isn't she?' Dad says to me with a nod.

The other paramedic, a brown-haired giant with bulging arms, turns to us. I feel small under his intense gaze. 'We need to move your dad down the stairs. We can't carry him. He will have to walk.'

Dad shouts that he will be unable to do this and lobbies for more drugs. 'I need strong sedative,' he says. 'Please give me strong sedative.'

The woman paramedic returns, speaking in a hard and clear voice. 'Mr Nour, if you can make it down the stairs, we have some lovely anaesthetic waiting for you in the ambulance.'

Dad ignores her ultimatum, negotiating instead with the man in blue, saying, 'You will have to carry me. I'm too weak.'

Eventually, Alan – the name of the giant, which Dad obtains by asking many personal questions, including 'Do you have kids?' and 'How would you like someone to treat your sick father?' – gently ushers Dad down the steps. Alan is bearing most of Dad's weight on his beefy arm.

Dad is laid out on a stretcher, which takes him to the ambulance waiting outside. A few puffs of the anaesthetic hose make him smile and then descend into a round of dry retching. A long string of saliva dribbles out the side of his mouth.

He winks at Mum and I weakly and says, 'We need to find out what this is so I can use it later.'

~

Five hours on, with Dad now asleep in his hospital bed, we are visited by a doctor who places some scans into an illuminated frame on the wall.

'It looks like your father has suffered a small stroke,' he says. 'Also, a collapsed L4-L5 disc, because there is no cartilage between these vertebrae.' The doctor points to the X-ray.

I nod, pretending to understand.

Mum turns to Dad with narrowed eyes, seething with rage and prodding him awake. 'You are a silly man! Why didn't you say that your back hurt this badly?!'

Dad is moved from the emergency ward to a regular room, where he stays for two weeks. Though we are told he cannot receive more than two visitors at any one time, it does not stop us from sneaking twelve people into the room that he shares with three other patients.

There are so many of us that we spill through the curtains

separating the beds: Tant Carmen and Uncle Kareem, Shoukry and Ayman, cousin Layla and Hussein and their son, Matthew. The old white man in the bed next to Dad's looks like an emaciated Santa Claus, with a long white beard and bony knees propped up beneath the hospital sheets. He is playing Uno with our little cousin Hany.

The men are watching Arsenal play Liverpool FC on SBS Sport. Dad speaks up to remind everyone what an incredible winger he was, playing the field with speed and alacrity. 'I could hit the goal from the other side of the pitch!'

I see him now, shrunk down in size, looking so weak and vulnerable in his state-issued hospital sheets and gown. I remember how I would lay my head against the tufts of hair swirling in circles on his forearms and at the base of his neck as a child. I could hear the sound of his heart, sure of its constant *galumph, galumph, galumph*. Now, he reminds me of an injured player who has to be whisked off the pitch after a game goes awry.

'Everybody has to leave now!' shouts the nurse, Fawzia, whom Layla says she recognises from her delivery at Liverpool Hospital years earlier.

In response to his complaints that the hospital diet is plain and depressing, Mum has equipped Dad with kofta sandwiches, vulgar with the stink of rendered beef fat and grassy cumin. She places them in the top drawer of his hospital bedside cabinet before leaving – precious contraband safely stored. Fawzia pretends not to notice this infringement because she also probably hates white bread with margarine and Vegemite.

Dad returns home the next week. He is fine for a while, enjoying the remedial massages that the hospital has organised.

A small Filipina physiotherapist comes to visit him today. 'Hello, Mr Nour!' she shouts in a shrill, jubilant voice. I have already turned him onto his stomach, in readiness for his treatment.

She lifts his blue flannelette pyjama shirt, revealing the leathery expanse of his lower back, then rubs a greyish-blue ointment, unctuous and nasal-opening, deep into his sciatica-affected spine. He shouts in agony, with deep guttural groans.

Though Dad can move his feet, which the doctors insist is a good sign, he is told that only surgery will assist in the long-term journey towards self-sufficiency. He is placed on a waitlist and told that they will confirm available sessions in a few weeks.

The next month and a half is hell ... for me in particular. Dad's a drainer at the best of times, but now there's the added bonus of a stereo effect with his constant yelling.

'Leh ya Rab, leh? Ana kont kwayes embara7! Laken mish ha2olak leh, ha2olak shokran!' Dad shouts. 'Why, God, why? I was fine yesterday! But I won't ask why! I shall say thank you!'

I wish he wouldn't say anything at all, especially at three in the morning, which is usually when the night painkillers he takes have worn off, leaving him vulnerable to spasms of shocking pain and us to more nightmarish bouts of screaming. Mum occasionally says, 'Khalas, Fareed!' from the other room (they no longer share a bed) and this quietens him down for a while.

When it all becomes too much, I call his GP, who organises a private stay at the good hospital in the city for a laminectomy.

'He needs to have bone shaved around the vertebrae,' Dr Suresh tells me on the phone, with the ease of someone talking about pruning an overgrown bush.

An ambulance arrives to take him to a private facility with a physiotherapy pool, as well as a dedicated surgical theatre. Dad spends the night before his early-morning surgery getting to know the other men in his hospital room. They are a Greek and a Pole. Spyros complains to Dad of his lousy kids, who no longer visit him after the messy divorce he had ten years prior, and Jakob doesn't say much of anything because he is so weak. Still, Dad likes to sporadically shout encouraging, vaguely Christian statements at him like, 'God is the greatest, Jake!'

They all talk of soccer. 'What did you think of Ronaldo in that match against Manchester?' Dad asks Spyros. 'He's a big show-off! All dance but no skill.' Jakob looks on, silent and intense.

The day after the surgery, Mum visits him with more food. This time it is chicken skewers wrapped in Lebanese bread with sumac and onion. The doctor comments that he has performed many laminectomies before but has seen few nerves as severely impacted as Dad's. Dad tells Dr Suresh of the twelve years he spent laying electrical wire at Telecom and the other ten years running his mixed business, lugging heavy boxes of magazines and groceries from trucks and unpacking them onto shelves.

Now is the time for Dad's long course of physiotherapy. A nurse walks him through his paces.

'Hello, Mr Nour,' Liam declares. 'Look at you, getting all big and strong now and looking so handsome.' Liam winks at me and my cheeks flush red with self-consciousness.

'Hmmm,' Dad concedes, disgruntled by the man's campness.

At the rehabilitation clinic, Liam walks dad through a series of exercises: some on a flat bed, such as pelvic tilts, inner range quads and static quad raises; others performed between two parallel bars, requiring Dad to support his own body weight while performing calf raises. Dad struggles, lumbering like Jesus has commanded him to 'walk again'.

'Come on, big man, you can do it!' Liam shouts encouragingly.

A fortnight later, when Dad completes the exercise unassisted, he accepts a hug from Liam.

'Liam, I was a star on the pitch when I played soccer for Egypt,' Dad says. 'When I came here in '69, they said it was just a sport for wog boys.'

Liam nods patiently.

Three weeks later and before discharge, Dr Suresh returns to talk to Dad. 'Mr Nour,' he says, 'you've had a very serious surgery. You have to change your life completely. The physiotherapy that you're doing must continue long after you leave this hospital. No heavy lifting or pushing on anything. No lifting anything at all for a while, actually, and then nothing over 20 kilograms. Your diet must change. You need to reduce your sodium, eat four to five cups of fruit and vegetables every day, and above all, exercise.

Every day you need to exercise for at least thirty minutes.'

Dad nods, taking the doctor's hand and shaking it. 'Please read this, Suresh,' he says, scrabbling through the cabinet next to his bed and passing the doctor a pamphlet with the words, 'Saved for eternity in a moment of time.'

~

A few months into Dad's recovery, cousin Ayman comes over for dinner. He has just returned from a long trip to Egypt, where he went to buy lots of cheap tobacco and shisha pipes for his hookah shop. He and Dad are watching soccer.

'Ah, that's a foul! A foul!' Dad shouts. 'No need for a red card like that!' Then he turns to Ayman, his eyes wide in wonder. 'I used to play so well. I could run for hours. I could bend the shot on penalty and win the whole match.'

'No running for you now, Uncle,' Ayman answers.

When we move back to the TV room after dinner, Ayman opens a suitcase to reveal small gift bags, marked with the names of my aunts and uncles in Egypt.

I get three cotton singlets, some souvenir playing cards with the bust of Tutankhamun, the severely disabled king, and a fake-leather wallet. Rita and Mum get some stockings and a skin-lightening product called 'Fair and Lovely' respectively. The gift bag made out to Dad contains three knock-off colognes in plastic bottles called 'Yves Saint Cordon', 'Bucci' and 'Calvin Klean'. There is also Colonoscol, an Egyptian-only laxative tablet. On the phone with Mum last week, Aunty Huda insisted from her Cairo apartment that this would help Dad to pass a stool 'very, very easy, like butter.'

I'm more interested in the outside of the gift bag. It is made of a shiny plastic and bears the image of Leonardo DiCaprio and Kate Winslet, an azure sky behind them and the pink of the setting sun on Kate's dress as she falls into Leo's embrace on the ship's bow. It says in huge italicised golden font across the front of the stern, 'My heart is go on!'

How to Be a Big TV Star

The wise man savours his bread in quiet, while the fool scatters crumbs in the village square.

I stride into the youth group viewing party with the swagger of a conquering hero, channelling the spirit of Salah ad-Din post-Crusades or Pope Urban rallying his troops for battle. The air feels tingly with anticipation as we gather for this special 'movie night' – the TV premiere of the reality documentary series I'm in, *Christians Today*. Pride gleams in the eyes of my fellow parishioners at Our Lady of the Holy Cross and I feel a surge of excitement coursing through me as we chant our Lord's praises in unison: '*Kyrie Eleison, Kyrie Eleison, Christe Eleison.*'

During the chorus of voices, I send a text to my friend Marty, a connection at a TV production company I want to join – a subsidiary of Yahoo7 and Vice News. It's my dream job.

'Can't wait for you to see the show, man. I think I really shine in it,' I message eagerly.

Marty responds quickly, his enthusiasm palpable even through text. 'Wouldn't miss it, mate.' His reassurance echoes the confidence he instilled in me last week over coffee when he assured me that I was a shoo-in for a gig as a researcher at Special Broadcasting Services investigative news series called *Foresight*, that it was just a matter of signing the contract.

I remember what Father Constantinos told me a year ago when the phone call first came in to do the TV show. 'Habibi, I think you should do this. I think you should take this opportunity to defend our church and its teachings against all the fake news out there.'

Looking up to Christ hanging off the cross, I whisper a prayer of thanks for his faithfulness. My heart feels heavy with the thought of Judas' subtle betrayal, the sweet kiss that marked out an innocent victim, but the SBS logo is now playing on the TV and I put it out of my mind. My head feels light with excitement.

My big face fills up the screen, and I see myself staring earnestly down the barrel of the camera. 'Marriage is a sacred institution established by God,' the Daniel on screen pronounces in a huff, his maroon shirt 'popping' against the blackened room. 'It's and what God has made, man cannot unmake or alter.' Onscreen Daniel clutches nervously at his pant leg while a vein throbs on his temple.

The statement gets cheers and applause from my youth group, as well as an 'Amen, brother!' The whirring of a fan in the corner of the youth hall reminds me of the gentle whirring of the air conditioner in the SBS production room six months earlier.

'Daniel, we really want an authentic Arab Christian voice out there,' Keely the production manager said to me, the talent. She stared at me, laser-focused, and propped up on a stool, her Botox-frozen brow tilting in what I assumed was an expression of concern. Three cameramen moved around me in a synchronised dance, a gentle breeze swaying the black tarp of the background fabric. One of them shut the door with a bang, the room shuddering.

'So tell me,' she continued, 'what do you *really* think of gay marriage?' Keely pursed her duck lips expectantly, waiting for my answer.

I launched in, a Coptic Catholic soldier fighting to single-handedly right the wrongs of a morally bankrupt society with nothing but the Holy Spirit, some rosary beads for a necklace and a maroon shirt from Connor. Society needed Jesus, and I was about to give Him to them.

'Marriage is between a man and a woman, and anything else is an abomination – case closed,' I said calmly.

The next day I was in an Uber to Bella Vista in Sydney's West, where a group of ten Christians would be cooped together in a place that would later be described by narrator Anthony Griffis as 'the heart of Australia's Bible Belt' to discuss hot-button issues. As I exchanged greetings with the other housemates, C-grade Australian TikTokkers for Christ, I could hear Rita in my ear: 'Are you sure you want to do this, bro? You're hardly the poster child for being a good Christian boy. You're a bit fruity.'

But it was too late for all that now. We sat down to have

our first dinner of the show. I was treading water here, between fundamentalist evangelicals on one side and progressive hippies on the other, and if I looked down, even for a moment, I would sink. Things quickly got tense at the dining table during dinner.

'What the Church is doing to gay people is wrong!' Chris, the Pentecostal conversion therapy survivor, shouted from his chair at the head of the table.

Chris was thin and very pale and wore a cap over his bald head, which cast a constant shadow over his blue eyes. He asked everyone seated, one-by-one, if they would sign his petition to stop conversion therapy in churches. The two evangelicals, Surendra and Tim, looked down and away. Andrew the Baptist said, 'Well, we should still have the right to teach our beliefs without judgement from others.' Jo and Tiffany, the two woke lefties, said that it was wrong that this still happened, wrong to tell a teenager that their sexual orientation could change with a bit of faith and effort. Lucy the Mormon cried, 'Gay people have the hardest cross to bear' with a broken voice. I swallowed hard when everyone looked my way, awaiting my response. I shook my head a bit in what I thought seemed like an expression of general concern. Videographers ducked and swerved, like hyenas around a carcass or the cameramen at a top 1 per cent OnlyFans production.

The next day, we went to an evangelical church service at the Streetside Chapel, a service meant for Asian international students studying at Sydney universities.

Pastor Alan Chan rose to the pulpit to address a crowd of Chinese and Korean twenty-year-olds. 'Welcome to RICE ministry. A chance to share good food and good faith!' The crowd swelled with whoops and yells. 'Are you ready to get riced? Are you ready to hear the song of victory?'

On the wall next to me was the RICE charter, an acronym that stood for Rest in Christ, In the ministry, Charismatic faith and Excellence. It felt like they phoned that last one in a bit.

'Yes, Daddy Lord, yes, Daddy Jesus,' Pastor Alan prayed, hands up in the air and mouth on the microphone. 'It's time to hear the gospel message, church.'

The audience moaned their assent. 'Yes, hmmm, amen, Lord.'

A song called 'Come to Jesus' blasted through the speakers while Pastor Alan threw a bucket of dry rice into the audience. 'Wherever the good seed is planted, it yields a hundredfold!' he shouted, and a bit of rice fell down my collar: teppanyaki for Christ.

Catholic Janet rolled her eyes but everyone else was right into it, swaying along with the music, including the Mormon girl, her long hair falling down to her waist, her toes showing through her sandals.

'I used to go to stuff like this,' Gay Chris said. 'I performed for the church band, but then I made out with the minister's son backstage and they had me barred from service, which was funny because the band was called Brothers in Christ.'

The next morning at the breakfast table, it was confessional time. Keely leaned over us, her brow vibrating under some kind of inner pressure. She said that she would like us all to say something 'honest about our struggles'. Then her forehead snapped back to factory settings, a smooth expanse once more.

First up was Gay Chris: 'They told me that the reason I liked men was because I had a fractured relationship with my father, that my mum was overbearing and that the Holy Spirit could help heal this wound.'

Cassandra, the Uniting Church gyno, was next: 'Yes, I perform abortions, but that doesn't mean I'm a bad person. I just don't believe that bringing a baby into this world is always the right decision.'

Andrew the Baptist: 'When we started Lifeline Church, I didn't realise that the head minister was using all the money to extort parishioners, avoid taxes and buy a private jet.'

On and on the litany of offences went. Tiffany had been felt up by a creepy priest, Tim was told he was too Chinese-looking to be on the church YouTube channel, Jo's sister wanted to be a nun but was flatly denied because she had a kid out of wedlock, Surendra's mum hadn't spoken to him in years since he converted out of Hinduism, and Lucy was mad that other Christians thought Mormons weren't true believers because of differences in the creed.

They all turned to me. It was my turn to say something shocking. I felt a pressure building around my temples. This had to be good. I blurted out that my family had been persecuted by the Muslim Brotherhood in Egypt and threatened with death, and that was why we now lived in Sydney. This wasn't true –

Gidoo had moved here on a migrant visa to work at CityRail in the late 60s. Lucy was glassy-eyed, Andrew was shaking his head. Cassandra turned to me, took my hand and said, 'I want to hold you.' The cameraman lingered over the distraught look on her face. I was frozen, incapable of forming a coherent response.

Later, after being filmed brushing my teeth so that the production team could get enough overlay for the episode, I finally had a few moments of privacy. A torrent of tears came gushing out as the impact of my lie took its toll on me. I felt like a sellout, throwing my fellow Arabs under the bus to please all these self-righteous white people. Gay Chris came in and saw me crying.

'I'm so ashamed,' I blubbered.

'You shouldn't be ... It's not your fault they attacked your family like that.' He drew me into a hug, his hands tight and strong around my back.

I abruptly pulled away, wiping my eyes. 'It's fine. I know it's not my fault ... It's fine.'

He was smiling at me but there was something concerned, or maybe confused, in his blue eyes.

I went to wash my face in the bathroom and when I emerged, Chris confronted me.

'How can you still be spouting that old-school stuff about marriage being just for a man and a woman? Honestly, get with the times. It's backwards to say that today.'

I said I was entitled to my opinion and he walked off to dinner, his brow furrowed.

Back to the dark room the next day and it was time for me to launch my defence of traditional Christian values. I roped my rosary beads around my neck, touched my scapular beneath it and prayed the Jesus Prayer: 'Jesus Christ, Son of God, have mercy on me, a sinner.' I walked in with the conviction of Meryl Streep in *Doubt*, about to get the paedophile priest fired, or at least moved to a different parish for a while.

'I see society all around me devolving, basing itself on humanist values that can't really take us anywhere. Faith isn't just some optional add-on in life; it's the whole foundation,' I began.

Keely's eyes widened, impressed and maybe a bit scared by my holiness. I felt like Moses coming down the mountain, face alight with glory.

'These days everyone talks about being spiritual but not religious, or believing in humanity but not in God. I just don't accept that. Without God, we're like a ship without a compass. Without faith, life's just a random series of events, with no rhyme or reason.'

I thought of the painting my parents hung in their house, of a sailor steering a ship through a storm, a white, blue-eyed Jesus with one hand on the young man's shoulder and the other divine hand pointing to safe harbour.

'When times get tough, where's humanism? Nowhere to be found. Sin abounds, people do whatever they want and say they're "living their truth". But their truth fails them and they are alone and depressed in the end.' A bubble exploded somewhere inside me and I felt simultaneously deflated and elated. 'But faith? It's there, offering comfort, support and a whole community of like-minded believers. So, yeah, call me old-fashioned, but I'll take faith over humanism any day of the week.'

The buffed interiors and bouclé couches of the Bella Vista mansion transform into the high arches and austere pews of Our Lady of the Holy Cross, and suddenly I'm back at church. The show has gone to commercial: Eurovision is airing next week and the presenters are camp in feathers and ruffs.

Before I can hear them, I am embraced by the youth group. Thirty youth are standing up all around me, clapping and cheering. Father Constantinos wipes a tear from his eye. I get pats on the shoulder, admiring looks from the boys.

Father speaks up. 'Habibi, you did us proud. You took an opportunity to defend our church and its teachings against all the evil propaganda out there.' More applause.

A ping on my phone – a message from Marty at the TV production company.

'Dan, really sorry, mate, but I don't think you're what we're looking for in this gig. We work with lots of diverse communities and have a pretty open perspective. You may not be the best fit.'

I am rushed outside, carried by the momentum of the crowd. Around me cans of Coke Zero are being cracked open, plump sausages slammed into bread rolls. But I am not there. I think of poor Judas who killed himself from shame. Nobody celebrates Judas.

How to Date Men

A brother in need is a brother indeed.

We all sit down to a meeting of 'Brown Allies, Relatives and Friends', or BARF. Two closeted older men with receding hairlines are seated in the circle of chairs in the dingy basement. The air is listless and stolid in the summer heat.

Every cell of my body rejects the experience of being here. How can I be thirty and so deep in the closet? I'm on the same leaky lifeboat as Rajesh, a fifty-two-year-old Indian father of four, and Charbel, a Lebanese doctor who still lives with his judgemental Catholic mother. The captain of our vessel is a big burly Yogi Bear of a man called Barry, who talks so camply that I feel the tingly flush of shame creep into my neck whenever he flaps a limp wrist.

Please don't ask me to speak, I think, pinching the pad of my thumb with my other thumb to steady myself. I begin to feel dizzy in the heat. Aren't the gays supposed to be good at interior design? Can't they afford a fan?

'... and that's when my father said, "If you ever bring a man home, better you die." Then he had a heart attack, the paramedics couldn't revive him and *he* died,' Rajesh finishes. Charbel shakes his head and Barry nods sincerely, a little smile on his giant face.

'Thank you, Rajesh, so, so powerful,' Barry says, placing his big gay hand on his heart and dropping his head like a Miss World contestant. 'Daniel, try topping that! Oh ... haven't I heard that before?' He laughs at his naughty joke. 'No, honestly, tell us what brings you here today.'

I summon my nerve, suck in my tummy and straighten up. 'Last month I was on a TV show criticising gay marriage, but I think I might be, you know, that way inclined ... and I feel kind of bad about it?'

A look of comprehension spreads across Barry's face; I reckon he might have seen me soapboxing about family values on *Christians Today*.

I feel sudden anger creeping up my spine. 'But in my defence, you know, everyone encouraged me to do it and if I didn't, they might have known I was, you know, that way inclined.'

'Gentlemen, let's just say gay from now on – there's no shame in that,' Barry interjects with a smile. Charbel jumps in, swarthy of face and giant of nose, to explain that actually there's a lot of shame in being called gay in the Middle East and that the word gay itself is a slur in many Arab countries.

'Well, here, gay is A-okay,' Barry continues, inviting Charbel to 'say more about that'. I'm annoyed that the mic has been taken away from me so suddenly.

Charbel explains that he fled Lebanon during the civil war with his uncle. Determined to make something of himself, he worked tirelessly at a fruit grocer in Punchbowl, earned his medical entry certificate and eventually opened his own GP clinic. He even managed to ship his mother over from Tripoli to live with him in Baulkham Hills, where she now spends her days watching Lebanese soap operas and criticising his cleaning.

'I could never come out to her. It would kill her. Honestly, it would put her right in the grave,' he says, shaking his head. 'She still thinks I'm going to marry the girl from the church choir – she's already married with two kids, but you can't tell my mother that.'

'We promise we won't, Charbel. We promise we won't.' Barry extends his tree-limb arm ending in branched fingers and holds Charbel's tiny fist.

The rage has returned, bubbling around my chest: I need to speak up, I need to expunge this guilt. I need to redeem myself.

'Barry, I'd really like to know if there's a way I can feel less embarrassed with … guys … I mean, gay guys.' I gulp and continue. 'I don't feel confident enough to go out to clubs or bars or anything because what if they say, "Hey, aren't you the guy from that show?"'

Barry tells me he thinks this probably won't happen, and Rajesh and Charbel implore me to 'give it a go', saying I am young and can start afresh. If this was *Life of Pi*, I'd have killed them all by now and eaten them for nourishment. Nevertheless, I take their advice, and that night I steel myself with a few shaky breaths before perusing Fumble and Hinge. I consider a stream of profiles on these apps, only to find that they are all the same: a parade of ripped torsos, gym selfies and 'masc4masc' bios. My heart sinks. I'm Arab, I'm stocky – and let's face it, most of these guys are looking for the same thing: white, shredded, dead in the eyes. My own preference for white guys, with whom I feel more anonymous than the brown gays who all gossip, doesn't exactly help my case.

That's when I come across Jordan, dapper with an edge of danger: his bespectacled face says private-school boy, and his earring and tattoo say Oxford Street at two in the morning. His pictures are refreshingly normal. No thirst traps, no moody black-and-white poses – just him with an easy grin in front of popular tourist destinations like Angkor Wat and the Eiffel Tower. He has an air of worldliness. A traveller.

I swipe right, generating a 'nuzzle', and he responds in turn with a 'bite'.

I tell him about my predilection for white guys, thinking I should probably lay my cards out early. 'I know – it's a whole complex,' I message him. 'Add it to the therapy list.'

A pause. Another beat that feels like an eternity. Will he leave me on read like all the others? Then he LOLs, and a wave of relief sweeps through me.

Jordan feels different from the usual. In our chats, we don't dance around anything. We talk about the pressure to look perfect. I tell him what it's like growing up Arab in Sydney and he confirms that he thinks Western Sydney culture is more an aesthetic than an ethnicity.

Finally, after three weeks of back and forth, I walk into the Marrickville Hotel on a sticky summer night, heart pounding, hoping the guy I've been spilling my guts to online lives up to the image I've built in my head.

Jordan greets me with a big hug, removing his light jacket. He smells woody and sweet. His eyes are kind, and he sits on the stool in front of me, relaxed. I order a vodka sunrise. He orders a negroni. We talk about everything: he was christened Catholic but thinks of himself as more of a 'humanist'. After getting his political science degree, he made money as an au pair taking care of snooty Parisian kids, then did a gap year in London.

'After Europe, I did mission work across the Caribbean and heaps of South America; I worked in an orphanage in Lebanon and then on a farm in Canada with my cousin for a while.' He talks fast and orders me another drink.

Later, we share pad thai and beef massaman curry at Thai Pothong Restaurant in Newtown. Things are going so well that I don't hesitate to invite him back to our place to 'relive the drama of *The OC* – maybe a few episodes, maybe the whole first season'. With Mum and Dad at church camp and Rita at a girlfriend's place, I know we won't be interrupted. Jordan smiles, rolling his eyes at my overly enthusiastic pitch.

Driving down the M5 in my Kia Cerato, we listen to Kylie and Madonna. We ascend the stairs of the front porch in silence, and once inside, he compliments our Bankstown two-storey. I light a patchouli-scented candle and turn the dimmer, setting the lights low and warm, then offer him some red wine from Aldi I found in the pantry, pouring it into a thin plastic flute. He knocks it back in one gulp.

I flick the TV on and the SBS nightly news bulletin plays. Jordan's shoes are already off and I join him on the couch where he immediately grabs my thigh. He turns his head to me. His lips are freshly chapsticked and gleaming.

Gripping the back of my head, he pulls my face to his lips. He kisses me long and deep, exploring my mouth with his tongue. I push him down onto the couch, laying him flat. I'm hungry, my heart is sore and desperate, my eyes are wide with longing. I pull off his shirt and gently kiss his Adam's apple, moving down to the glistening hollow at the base of his neck. Then I lick my way down to his belly button, where blond hairs poke out of the waistband of his Bonds underwear.

That's when it happens. Out of the corner of my eye, I see someone who looks and sounds just like me on the TV screen. He is in a maroon shirt. The vein on his temple is throbbing. He is clutching his pant leg. The caption reads, 'Daniel Nour, Coptic Christian'. I hear myself confidently say, 'Marriage is between a man and a woman, and anything else is an abomination – case closed.'

Jordan turns to see why I've stopped tonguing him.

'Hey, isn't that you?'

How to Survive a Global Pandemic

In disaster's path, forsake thy family.

'It's the Chinese!' declares my racist uncle, Kareem. 'They invented it in a lab and they pumped it into rats and chickens because they knew it would shut down our schools and ruin the whole country.' When Kareem shouts, his small, beady eyes come popping out of his lids, a vein enlarges around his neck and he turns a bit green.

When I first heard on the news that there was a contagious disease in the population, I thought it might be a short-lived kind of thing. That was eighteen months ago. Now I know that we must live with the virus and a new culture of social distancing, mask-wearing and generalised restraint.

Dad was the first to notice this new turn of events when he heard Donald Trump discussing a 'China virus' on the news. 'The novel coronavirus is sweeping through Wuhan, China,' the reporter said, while Dad filled out a sudoku puzzle in the free community newspaper *Senior Life*. 'Chinese authorities have closed off the city of Wuhan by cancelling planes and trains leaving the city and suspending buses, subways and ferries within it.'

Though my office job at the *Inner West Courier* offered the possibility of leaving the house for a couple of days, Dad refused to concede. 'Home is where the heart is. Home is where you will be safest. The trains are full of sickness.'

Despite his insistence that this was a time for prudence, Dad seemed to go out a lot. Even though he had survived the Arab–Israeli War of Attrition, he became weak when he saw the 'reduced for clearance' stickers at Aldi. He would return home bearing loaves of focaccia and Turkish and Lebanese bread, beaming. He would also produce several large, plump chickens and racks of beef ribs. Though we were vegetarian for Lent, we all nodded encouragingly.

The 24/7 nature of the emergency spoke to Dad's deep need to know what was going on. With his brother in Cairo, a man with similarly maudlin sensibilities, he discussed all the sombre realities of this disease at length on nightly Viber calls.

'All those people on the cruise ship that docked at the harbour full of disease?' Dad said to my uncle Merhom. 'Dead.'

'All the hospitals here, riddled with disease.' Merhom responded, waiting for the words to settle. 'The streets here in Shubra, full of disease ...'

'These are the dark days written in scripture,' Dad added.

A month later and Sydney was in full lockdown. We were

told that we could not leave the house for anything other than essential grocery shopping. Public parks and pools were closed or cordoned off. Family on Mum's side lost their work in shopping centre security; on Dad's side, my meathead cousins Shoukry and Ayman said they were taking time off until the lockdown lifted but were actually busy trading bitcoin and, in Shoukry's case, finishing a house-arrest sentence. Nothing much had changed for Shoukry.

With this news, my father launched into a full atavistic refugee mentality. News footage of two women frantically fighting over a twelve-pack of toilet paper at the local grocery store was the straw that broke this camel's back, or at least damaged it further since Dad's back is already kind of broken since his double laminectomy. Dad sprang up from his chair, lunged for his wallet and made for the car.

While Dad emptied the supermarket shelves of toilet paper, which was unnecessary because all the toilets in our house had built-in bidets, Mum came across naturopathic remedies while scrolling Facebook, which she insisted would help us get through this era of deathly infection.

Her suggestions for curing the virus included:

boiled betel leaves, which she found at the Indian grocer down the road
lemon and salt water
a herbal drink containing ground turmeric, ginger, black pepper and honey
Panadol

There was a strange quality to this pandemic: technically, we knew that time must be moving, for we saw the green foliage turn orange and then drop to the floor, yet there was also a kind of perpetual stasis.

'It's like purgatory,' Rita told Mum.

'That's only for Catholics,' she responded while stirring a pot full of molokheya.

Mum took to the task of housework with all the zeal of the woman in the Book of Proverbs, of whom it is said, 'She seeketh wool, and flax, and worketh willingly with her hands … She riseth also while it is yet night, and giveth meat to her household, and a portion to her maidens.'

Though Mum didn't have any maidens, she was consumed with the repetition of tedious cookery. She spent her days stuffing vine leaves with rice and carefully rolling them up like tight little Cuban cigars; wrangling enormous traybakes of penne and minced beef stewed in tomato and laced with hot bechamel sauce into the oven; and pickling onions, capsicum, lemon and cucumber to varying degrees of sourness.

I was also busy, taking the same route on foot around the neighbourhood twice daily. I ate three meals a day without fail and called all my friends on the phone, in the misguided hope that doing so would make them appear before me or do something to bridge the distance between us. I also checked the mailbox multiple times a day, even though mail only arrived once in the morning, and even then, it was usually only an Aldi brochure.

In lieu of actual haircuts – all the barbershops were closed – I had to learn how to self-groom. A good fade was very important, so I bought a shaving kit online to give myself and Dad a cut by adjusting the trimmer settings. I took too much off down the middle of my head, making me look like a reverse Pepé Le Pew. That was when I decided to shave all the remaining hair off. When I went downstairs, Mum asked me why I looked like I was joining the army: there was no conscription in this country. Cutting Dad's hair was easier because he didn't have any on top, so I just trimmed a bit off his semicircle tonsure and called it a day. He looked like Saint Francis of Assisi, which is ironic because he hates vegetarians.

I was not allowed to see the friends I missed, but I couldn't escape my immediate family. Before the pandemic, Rita and I would avoid our parents most of the time, except for the drive with Dad to and from the train station for work every day. Now they were before us all day long. I would walk downstairs from my bedroom for a break from a two-hour work meeting on 'online synergies' and find my dad sitting in the kitchen scrolling conspiracy theories on Facebook. I would go outside and find Mum pulling up weeds near the mint plants. I would go back upstairs to use the bathroom and find that it was occupied by Rita, who was playing Fifth Harmony's 'Work from Home' from behind the door. Then it would be time for the next work meeting on 'corporate intersectionality'.

Mum rolls and flattens, kneads and bakes tray upon tray of kahk, and Dad spends a lot of his time ironing tea towels. Time folds in on itself like one of those cheap Chinese hand fans that Mum would use to cool herself when Father Constantinos' homily was droning on too long during summer. Then, a sudden respite. Lockdown lifts long enough for us to meet at a house party at my cousin Layla's place in November 2021, which is supposed to be capped at twenty people and for which fifty show up.

I arrive with a sudden anxiety that feels like a tightness in my chest, like an overstuffed vine leaf ready to explode. My relatives and their friends ask me inane questions: 'How was it for you?' or 'Get up to much?' or 'Have you been on the dating apps?'

I don't know what to say about my stymied progress, that feeling of arrested development just as I was coming to terms with things, with my longings, my desire for love and companionship. I don't mention that I can't get that year back. Also, nobody speaks about my mum's uncle who died in Egypt because there weren't enough ventilators in the ICU in the coronavirus ward of a public hospital, or about the fact that everybody felt so lonely and afraid.

Many of those at the party are anti-vax conspiracy theorists. During the pandemic, they wrote on Facebook about how the vaccine was manufactured using the fetuses of aborted Christian babies and how the virus was foretold in the Book of Ezekiel. Now they say it's a good thing that the vaccine got out so quickly. My belly burns with frustration and I feel a bit nauseous at their hypocrisy.

When Rita and I get home, tense from the experiences of the last few hours and the last eighteen months more generally, we find our parents looking dour and serious in the living room. Dad tells us to sit down. There is a notebook and calculator on the coffee table.

'I don't have any money for you,' he begins. Mum nods seriously.

'We all have to go, kids. Every generation comes and goes.' Mum says in Arabic, looking up to God. 'You will need to take care of yourselves, look after your own needs and get married.' My sister wipes a tear from her eye. Dad coughs and then belches loudly. We decide to visit Costco.

How to Be a Spinster

Or How to Pass Your Use-By Date

An unmarried girl is her brother's duty, her mother's shame and her father's consolation.

Rita graduated from Sydney Uni with a Bachelor of Laws, she does taekwondo and spin classes, her tongue can kill and she's always dressed a little slutty. But because she is single, she is still not allowed to leave the house by herself.

This is the year that Mum has decided Rita must be wed. 'By Easter, we7yat Rabena. As God lives, either you will be married or I will be dead in the ground.'

Rita sneers, asking why she should be forced to marry when so many others remain single and perfectly content. With her sharp features and disdainful gaze, she looks like a velociraptor sizing up its prey. According to her, women only marry so someone can bail them out in a crisis, but with her lawyer's salary, she doesn't need a handout from 'some dodgy Arab's shady construction firm'.

'You're sitting at home on a Friday night, watching *Sex and the City* like a gronk,' I tell her. 'Even if you don't want to be married, at least put on some makeup and make an effort.'

'Shut up, you fuckin' bastard,' she snaps, her mouth twisting in disgust as she throws her arms up in a dramatic flourish. 'You look like an unwashed donkey's arse.' This is just some of the playful banter I enjoy with my older sister.

Because she is unmarried, I have to go with her to all social occasions. This is called wajib, meaning something like 'etiquette'.

'Go with her, habibi, ya Rab. Dear God, let her find the one. Introduce her to your friends.' Mum says to me with pleading eyes and open hands, appearing just now in Rita's doorway. Then she pulls me into the hallway by the arm, out of Rita's earshot. 'Habibi … if you can find someone for your sister to marry, I will make your baba pay for the new sneakers you wanted.' I can afford my own sneakers, but in this economy, I take the deal. Mum's weird bribe in mind, I head for the car. Rita trails behind.

Stepping into the Kia, Rita removes the knee-length shawl she is wearing to reveal a little black dress. She's been careful to evade Dad's gaze when she leaves the house ever since he saw a photo of her on Facebook in a tube top for her thirty-fourth birthday party and publicly commented, 'Forgive my daughter, she is dressed like a sharmoota' on her profile page.

Driving to 'Arabian Night' at House Bar in Darling Harbour, the only Arab-themed event in the city, I think more about

Mum's offer and what I can actually do to hook Rita up. I'm not sure if any of my friends will suit her. She thinks they have 'ESL-level communication skills' and that 'cuzzy' is not a term of endearment.

When we finally arrive at Darling Harbour, with Rita complaining that she has to walk the whole way in six-inch stilettos, we are greeted by my two mates from uni: Abanoub and Jawad. Abanoub is wiry and hairy; Jawad, whose name means 'horse' in Arabic, is tall, with a nose like a knife, and talks with an effeminate twang.

'Rita, you're looking great!' Jawad says. 'I love that dress on you.' He gives me an approving wink and nod, as though to indicate that he's very pleased with how much Rita has grown. Just as he tries to crack on to her, Rita walks over to her friends, rolling her eyes. Marina, Zainab and Stephanie are also in tiny dresses and surrounded by many small glasses and a half-empty bottle of Belvedere Vodka.

At the bar I overhear Rita say, 'There's no way I can tell Mum that I've been having sex. She even thinks a tampon can corrupt your purity.' The girls all shriek loudly, slapping their knees and clapping their acrylic-nailed hands.

I think it's funny but must pretend to be disapproving of Rita's alleged skankiness, because if it's made public it will dishonour the family. Jawad says he's 'totally obsessed' with what the girls are wearing, and the rest of us follow him over to their booth.

I hear Zainab's nasal shriek first. She is skinny, with a tightly stretched hijab and even tighter Gucci jeans. Zainab tells

Stephanie that since childhood her mother has told her that she should never greet her male friends with hugs and kisses. Stephanie, whose floor-length maxi dress covers her full figure, is wearing so much eye makeup that it gives her a panda-like look. Stephanie says that when she was a kid, her grandmother would tell her that when a girl and a boy are together in a room, the third guest is the devil. Rita says that both girls have been skanks since childhood and all of them laugh some more.

With my cold glass of Absolut peach-infused vodka in hand, I look at each of my mates in turn. They are so different. Would either of them be a good match for Rita?

Abanoub is trying to sip his whisky from a tall glass with a short straw. He is a corporate services accountant for a telco. We've known his family since back in the day. They're good people. His mum would send my mum plates of kahk and ba2lawa every Easter and he would come over to play Crash Bandicoot and secretly watch porn with me in Dad's office.

Abanoub is socially awkward – he accidentally kissed my mum on the lips at my teta's funeral because he's uncoordinated. Still, I try to concentrate on his talents. He did a TAFE course in 'Corporate Accounting 101' a couple of years back and since then has bought and renovated a duplex that he rents out to some Asians in Marrickville.

I tell Abanoub that Rita has always liked him, which is a lie. She only ever comments on his eczema, which is severe, and thinks it's weird that someone with so much property still lives with his mum. When Rihanna's 'Wild Thoughts' starts playing,

Rita hits the floor with her girls and Abanoub saunters over to crack on to her. It's hard not to laugh watching Abanoub try to get my sister's attention. He offers her his hand and she high-fives it.

Abanoub is gyrating alone now while the girls have started dirty dancing with some Brazilian guys they spotted on the floor. Rihanna is singing about getting nakey so that she can be her man's baby. Poor Abanoub really pulled the short straw tonight.

In the car ride home, I tell Rita that she should give Abanoub a proper chance. She objects, saying that it would feel like dating our father. I remind her of all the Egyptian soap operas that we watch with Mum, where the men are uniformly old and decrepit and the women young and cute. In one of these shows, a man marries a woman half his age and they take fun trips to amusement parks, where she stops him from eating konafa because she thinks he's too fat.

'He's not perfect, I know, but give him a go, you gronk,' I tell her one last time as we walk into the house.

Mum overhears, stomping out of the living room to confront my sister in the hallway. 'So, there was a boy? I see you coming and going all the time. Here your brother is, trying to connect you with some nice young man and you refuse.' Before Rita can cut Mum off, as she usually would, she is granted an ultimatum. 'If you give this boy a chance, I will stop asking you to marry.'

'Forever?' Rita asks, her eyes widening with incredulous hope.

'Yes, I will not ask you again … If you want to wilt and die on the vine, it is your choice,' Mum says with eyes downcast melodramatically.

~

Spying from behind the good room window, I see Abanoub pull up in his tricked-out Toyota Hilux. He steps out with slicked-back hair and gold chains gleaming over his half-open shirt, then opens the door for his small mum, who is wrapped in shawls. In his hand he clutches high-stemmed roses. Rita, also peering through the window in a little black dress, reminds me of the lambs that we raised at Gidoo's farm when the machete was being sharpened for Easter.

Mum is peering through the curtain of our formal room, the salon which is reserved for special guests. She sees Abanoub approaching, bouquet in hand. Alongside him is his tiny mother, who is wrapped in two huge shawls. She looks like a falcon, with sharply drawn eyebrows and a small beak nose. 'Open the door, you idiots!' Mum shouts. 'And please smile! For your mother's sake, smile!' She shoots a sharp glance at Rita.

'Ya hala, ya hala,' Mum says to the guests. 'Welcome, welcome to the son of goodness and the best of mothers.'

Abanoub fumbles to extricate his hand from the bouquet and shakes Mum's hand, pecking her on the cheek. He is wearing his signature cologne, Calvin Klein's Obsession. It makes my eyes water. He leans in to give Rita a kiss and, once again overshooting in his excitement, pashes her clean on the mouth. We all freeze. Nobody looks at anyone else in the eye for a few seconds.

Abanoub's mum breaks the silence. She tells him to stand straighter. 'Don't embarrass us in front of the bride.'

Mum erupts into high-pitched, silly laughter, like a schoolgirl. She loops her arm into Abanoub's, walking him into the good room. When everyone has sat down in the salon, where all the couches are embroidered in gold lace and everything is covered in tassels, Mum shoots another hard glance at Rita, who is perched on the edge of one of the nice chairs in the corner.

Taking her cue, Rita springs into action. 'Something hot or something cold?' she asks Abanoub.

'Oh, hot ... if it's not too much trouble ... or cold if you like ... Actually, Mum, what do you think?' Abanoub defers his choice to his mother with a sideways glance.

I can't look away from this tiny powerful woman and her big helpless man-baby. The mother tells Rita that he will have a cup of chamomile tea with honey because he has a runny nose.

After some chitchat about whether our teta left any money to Rita in her endowment, my sister returns with the tea and Abanoub's mother gets down to brass tacks. She covers everything, from how the wedding should be planned, to where the honeymoon should be, to where the home should be purchased. She also recounts a long list of Abanoub's allergies, including a rash he had on his left testicle when he was nine or ten.

At long last she concludes, 'So, as you can see, there are no problems here, ya Mama. I know you have been concentrating on the career and the professional stuff but now' – she raises her open palms to the heavens – 'it's time.'

Rita abruptly excuses herself into the kitchen and Mum follows.

I sit awkwardly with Abanoub. He looks like a big overfed emperor penguin chick and I feel sorry for him. Or is it that I'm embarrassed by him? Eventually, I decide that it's both.

Mum and Rita return to the salon. Everyone makes more small talk, this time about Gidoo's funeral fifteen years ago and whether the rumours that nobody was watching him at the time of his death were true. My phone buzzes and I see that Rita has sent me a WhatsApp message. It says, 'WHY THE FUCK AREN'T U HELPING, U GRONK? GET THIS LOSER OUT OF HERE.'

The mother now turns to me, her lips pursed. She may have finally got a read on this situation and that things aren't going her way.

'What do you think of all this, habibi?' she asks me.

Rita and Mum also turn my way. Abanoub too. In a vision, two competing options flash before me. The first is a pair of white New Balance sneakers, embossed in silver thread with a soft fabric weave at the toes. The other is Rita, veiled in white gauze and in a huge puffy white gown with giant billowy shoulders, crying bitterly.

'Um, maybe Abanoub needs to work on himself a bit more,

you know, like make some more money. Rita has very expensive taste,' I finally say, the $400 shoes vanishing out of my sight forever. His mother looks irate and I can feel Mum seething with rage from the corner.

I send an emergency text to Jawad later that night, once our guests have left and Mum and Rita have gone to their rooms in cold silence: 'Mate. Need your help. Rita rejected Abanoub – the gronk. Go out with her and I'll cover all your acai bowls this summer. Yalla bro.'

I feel like Jawad has a good chance. He's stylish, he keeps himself in good shape, he's in touch with his feelings – the kind of guy to post about Palestine and Black Lives Matter and Kendrick Lamar's new album.

Next morning, Rita tells me that Jawad asked her out and that he's taking her to a Japanese place in the city called Nobu. It serves very expensive food in very small portions. As it's a 'view to wed' kind of outing, Mum encourages it, a departure from her usual complaint that Rita spends way too much time out with other single girls: 'The blind leading the blind.'

But Rita returns early that night. It's not even 10pm when she walks in, interrupting our viewing of *El Hajj Metwalee's Wives*. Mum and I stare at each other quizically over a bowl of mixed nuts as Rita walks upstairs without a word. She summons me to her bedroom shortly after.

Rita sits down at her vanity while I stand at the doorway. Removing her makeup with a cotton pad, she huffs, 'Idiot, your friend is a homo.' She tells me that there were a lot of revelations on this date. Firstly, that Jawad has been to Japan. Secondly, that he went with his best friend, Sebastian. Thirdly, that he and Sebastian have shared not only great sushi but also their bodies and minds. I'm reeling a bit at the idea that Jawad, my homie, is a homo. At what this means for me. I feel embarassed and exposed, both at once. But I snap to, and focus on the issue at hand. Rita explains how he offered her a compromise. Jawad's parents are putting a lot of pressure on him to marry. Her parents are doing the same. So Jawad proposed that Rita become his beard, which is to say that they have a full wedding and accompany each other to public and family occasions but have a sister–brother relationship where they never have sex.

Rita says that Jawad was surprised to hear her say that there was nothing in this deal for her. 'I think he thought I was a lezzie. "But you like to travel, you're over thirty and not married, and you do taekwondo."' Rita told him that was to stay in shape and to 'cut a bitch' if some bastard ever cornered her in an alleyway.

Jaded from her experience, Rita takes a week off to join a yoga retreat, learning positions like downward-facing dog and warrior pose. Then she pours herself into work, sitting on a board for refugees and asylum seekers and being elected president of her Solicitors Alumni Network. She also starts learning to surf, driving all the way from Bankstown to Cronulla on Sunday mornings to take private lessons with a man called Jake, who I notice, standing shirtless on her Facebook wall, looks just like a Hemsworth brother.

By Easter, Rita decides to buy herself a new sheer dress with spaghetti straps. She saunters into her Solicitors Alumni Network cocktail party at Sydney Uni with a spring in her step. She even convinces Mum to come along, batting away her objections with, '3'ayari gaw shwaya, 3eshi 7ayatik! Change it up, live a little!'

After the canapes are eaten and all the niceties made, the vice-chancellor taps his champagne flute and motions to Rita to say a few words. 'Thanks, habibi,' she says, kissing him on the cheek. He smiles and blushes. She taps the microphone with her lacquered red nails, which are decorated with diamantes. 'Just checking that this is on.' Then she dives in, talking about our obligations to the 'disenfranchised' and to 'advocate for those members of society who have no voice'. She mentions that, as an Arab woman, she is proud to practise in a profession that often favours older white men. She thanks the university for hosting the party but says that it must do more to 'close the gap on inequality' by providing scholarships and remote learning programs for rural and Indigenous students. That's when Mum, smiling and nodding, turns to an old white man in a barrister's wig and forcefully whispers, 'That's my unmarried daughter!'

How to Come Out

Bury your secrets deep in the ground: to shame your father is worse than death.

It's one of our first family dinner parties after the pandemic. Uncle Kareem, Tant Carmen and Ayman all sit down in the salon, the Duke of Windsor suite. Mum brings out trays of tea and Lebanese sweets.

'Ayman has done very well – he has made it to the IT team at Google in the city. All the Google, all across Australia, he manages the IT for,' Kareem says of his eldest son, his eyes shining brightly.

'Congratulations to Shoukry for his engagement to the new girl! Why didn't you bring him and his 3arosa?' Mum asks Ayman.

'Shukran habibiti ... He couldn't make it, he had to work,' Tant Carmen shoots back before her son can respond. Now that Shoukry has been fired from the public service, we don't know what he does for work and Mum doesn't probe further.

'Danny too, when will he tie the knot?' Tant Carmen asks. 'Or is he too busy being a big TV star?'

In response, Mum looks up to heaven, hands outstretched in an expression of supplication.

'Soon, Insha'Allah,' Dad says, patting me on the shoulder. I feel the weight of his hand.

Stifled by the suffocating pressure of the room, I run upstairs, saying I have some emails to send, and call Father Constantinos.

A few weeks earlier, in the intimacy of the confessional, I told him my dark secret, the truth of my same-sex attraction. 'All my life, Father, now that I think of it. All my life,' I said, when he asked how long I had struggled with this. He didn't seem that surprised, especially after the debacle with Jennifer Eskander, my second cousin, whose brief romantic prospects with me flopped hard. He told me we 'all have our struggles' and recommended I say the Jesus Prayer with 'more contrition'.

Hearing Father's deep sonorous voice now, I imagine his face with its receding hairline and giant nose. I close my bedroom door, talking low to be sure that my family can't hear anything, and tell him that I feel bad for appearing on *Christians Today* to defend the Church's teachings on traditional marriage. He says it makes sense that I should feel torn about it. 'Everyone encouraged me to take a stand, Father. Like I had some moral duty,' I say. He tells me that my only duty is to myself and that I can always choose the 'middle path'.

This is new and I'm taken aback. I ask him what he means

and he tells me that I can still have gay relationships, go to confession and never tell anyone about it, and that 'that's what many of the clergy do'. I ask him if he thinks this is wrong. 'Son, the Church has changed its teachings on many things,' he begins. 'I could never have sex with a man myself, for example, and to be honest, I'd rather eat poo. But I'd watch, I'd be happy to watch.' I hang up abruptly. My head feels light. Everything I've been told is a lie.

When I come back downstairs, everyone has already left. Mum and Dad have washed all the dishes and are watching Egyptian TV. On NileSun is footage of the rainbow flag being waved at a 2017 Cairo performance of Lebanese band Mashrou' Leila, whose lead singer is gay. One of the concert attendees, Sarah Hegazi, was arrested and tortured for 'perversions against the state'. She killed herself in Canada shortly after her release.

'We are a religious society and this is against our values,' says the besuited Director of the Musicians Syndicate. He is in grey polyester and has a moustache that eats up a third of his pockmarked face.

Dad changes the channel to a flamboyant nine-year-old performing on *The Voice*. His mum is crying offstage. 'I'm so proud of him,' she says. 'I never want him to feel ashamed.'

Mum asks me if I'm still 'talking to' Rania, the latest church girl in whom she's taken an interest.

'I'm talking to everyone, Mum,' I say, tense and irritable. This is the last thing I need right now.

We keep watching the sissy boy sing his little heart out.

'You need to get yourself a wife,' Dad says.

My ears buzz. My heart stops and something inside me snaps. 'What if I don't want a wife?' I bark back. I'm surprised by my admission and the way that time stops, with my breath catching in my throat.

Mum and Dad both turn to me, stone-faced.

'What do you mean by that?' Dad eventually counters. 'If you don't want a wife, what do you want?'

We look at each other in silence.

Dad breaks it. 'Do you want ... a husband?'

The stare between us stretches into an eternity, although it lasts only a few seconds. The nine-year-old is still singing 'All by Myself' in a nasal shriek.

'I don't know what I want,' I tell him.

Dad's voice, now low and grave, matches his wide, terrified eyes. 'A man may come to you. An old man, a young man, whatever.' I think I know where this is going. I hope I am wrong. 'He will say come here and do this or come here and do that. Don't listen!'

I put my palm up. My chest is tight and my heart is thumping like a gazelle in flight. Dad stops abruptly and Mum looks down at her hands.

Later, after my shower, I find Dad outstretched on the couch. He is staring into space. I go back upstairs and into the overwhelming quiet. Even the crickets outside have fallen still.

How to Dance

A faffy boy is his mother's disgrace.

Tonight is the first night of the rest of my life. Tonight is elation. Tonight is freedom. Tonight is pleasure. Tonight I'm going to Stonewall on Oxford Street.

A dingy club with carpeted floors, Stonewall is so named for the Stonewall riots, which some people say started when a drag queen threw a brick and others say was down to vodka being too expensive.

In the upstairs bathroom of my home, I adorn myself with a sheer top studded with diamantes. My perky tits protrude a little under the heavy fabric. After raiding Rita's makeup counter, I carefully dot my eyelids with glitter and brush some shiny silver powder over the lids. Some gets in, stinging my eyes, and I immediately regret my mistake, wiping it off with a thin, scratchy towel. Like a Hallmark card, my therapist Barry's words come to me unbidden.

It's okay to feel pain. Just stay present.

I remember when I first started seeing Barry, who first convened the gay men's group therapy session I started three years ago. I had called him after falling into a shame spiral brought on by a hungry viewing of 'Arab men take it raw, doggy'. His bio said, 'Expert in therapy for culturally and linguistically diverse communities'.

Barry's office, part of a corporate shared space in Surry Hills, which takes an hour and a half to reach in peak traffic down the M5, was decorated with items that were eye-wateringly erotic. On a shelf on the wall, there stood a row of nine stone statues with huge protuberances that I first thought were noses but then realised were penises – like Easter Island Moai, but gayer. A large fresco of an Ancient Greek man gently lowering himself onto the erect penis of an older bearded man hung on the other side of the room.

'My mum's eyes are sad,' I told Barry pretty soon after we got to talking, my own eyes flitting across to the wall-porn. My words were met with a respectful silence. His face was soft and easy and his hands folded gently around his belly. I felt safe to continue. I explain how, since my bungled 'coming out' a few months ago, we've all tacitly agreed to carry on like it never happened.

Barry didn't console or patronise me. He asked good questions about why and for how long I had felt this way. He suggested that I could love my parents within healthy boundaries, in a way that didn't compromise my own happiness just to appease them. He asked if I might date someone, not just for the thrill of sexual adventure but for the possibility of finding someone to settle down with.

Over three months, he peeled me back like an onion – I cried raw, burning tears. Eventually the weeping stopped, but beneath it was a dull, hard sadness. Beneath this, the deeper and more turbulent magma flow of fear: the hellfire of the vengeful God. One of the ventures Barry set me on, the one that really tied my stomach in knots, was to go out to a club with no expectations and just have fun.

Tonight, I'm taking up his challenge. Reciting the comforting words he taught me like a litany – 'I am loved, I am safe, I am accepted' – I pull on my sluttiest pair of booty shorts and my cleanest white kicks. Then I cover it all up in one of Dad's old giant coats and run down the stairs and halfway down the street before my parents can shout out from the family room. Anyway, they are too deep into the episode of *El Hajj Metwalee's Wives* where he takes them all on a trip to Sharm El-Sheikh and the older ones get jealous of the younger's bikini bod.

I see my Uber driver, Hassan, and run towards his Mazda. Inside the car, the sound of prayerful recitation fills my ears. My eyes take in the miniature golden Qur'an stuck to his dashboard and the Shahada sticker on the windscreen behind me. I pull my coat around me a little tighter.

The streets fade from the greige of the suburbs to the vivid fluorescence of the inner city. I think back on all the confessions I gave to Father Constantinos in the musty sacristy over the last few months. I would jerk off to a porno that started with guys playing soccer and tell him I had 'acted out' after watching women's netball. I would ogle Brad Pitt's girthsome legs in *Troy* and tell him I had had 'impure thoughts'. Six months ago I had a wet dream after watching an episode of *Queer as Folk* and told him, 'The enemy is tempting me.' No more of that – no more confessing what is true to my nature, I remind myself, remembering Barry's admonition.

I am loved, I am safe, I am accepted, I tell myself again, releasing a new wave of nausea that threatens to engulf me.

All too soon, I arrive at the shameless pride flag that hangs over Stonewall. I step out onto the footpath, over a puddle and into the line out front, where people are flirting and laughing. With predictable conventionality, some are singing 'We're Off to See the Wizard', and a girl in a chequered blue miniskirt who looks about nineteen slaps the arse of her twink friend who, in lieu of clothes, is wearing a lion's tail over a golden jockstrap.

I pay my entry fee, have my hand stamped and walk into a laser show with heavy bass pulsing through giant speakers to the tune of Kylie's 'All the Lovers' and the alternatingly lustful and judgey stares of a thousand shirtless, chiselled gays.

My heart is pumping hard in my chest and I hear a buzzing in my ears that has nothing to do with the next song, the Sakgra remix of 'Real Groove'. I can feel sweat on my upper lip and my insides churning and bubbling. I am not cut out for this. What made me think I was?

Still in my coat and headed to the bathroom, I push aside a

dozen hairless torsos, past two guys deep-throating each other's tongues outside the bathroom door, and go into one of the cubicles. I sit down, fully clothed, on the toilet. My hands hold my head, which I slowly drop between my knees. My racing heart elicits a wave of queasiness, which I force down with all my might. I know that I must breathe slower, but in my panicked state I forget how. My heart races still faster and threatens to explode in my chest. My stomach turns yet further. Then, somewhere in the halls of my psyche, I hear the echo of Barry's deep voice.

You are loved, you are safe, you are accepted.

My sprinting heart slows down to a gallop, then a jog. I lift my head slowly, and it begins to clear. I open my eyes to see a flyer on the cubicle door: 'Friends of Dorothy: Jockstraps and Spellcraft'. Perfect, just perfect. Still, I have a choice to make: go home in shame or stay and shake my arse, which I have jammed into the white booty shorts I ordered online, and try to make the most of this.

Realising I have to get rid of Dad's giant burqa-like smock, I head over to Stonewall's rough-and-ready coat check. Behind the counter is a dark-eyed, wiry, lithe guy in a white ribbed singlet and green shorts. His brow is shiny with sweat and a mop of soft brown hair sits atop it.

'Hey, handsome, can I take that off your hands?'

It's a few seconds before I realise that he has asked me a question.

Flirt with the coat-check guy! I hear Barry say from down one of the shorter hallways in my psyche. *Say something clever, now, go!*

'That's not the only thing you can take off my hands.' I shake my head. 'Sorry, that's a very stupid thing to say.' Surprisingly, he smiles and shakes his head back.

Realising that a drink may help me think less and say something reasonable, I head to the bar. Jostling through the crowd of perky arses and V-shaped torsos, I eventually get the bartender's attention.

'What can I get you?' he shouts over the techno.

'A gin and tonic,' I say, as if by rote, remembering the time Rita told me I should stop ordering vodka sunrises because they made me seem like a pussy.

I sip my drink from a short straw, tasting the floral juniper and the acrid, sharp alcohol. That's when I see that the coat-check guy has joined the throng. I try not to look at him, but the effort just makes me look at him more.

Be relaxed, be straightforward, I hear Barry say from the living room in my mind, where he is sitting cross-legged and drinking Turkish coffee from one of Mum's tiny cups.

Coat-check guy is now standing beside me ordering his own drink. I side-eye him, trying to seem cool. He takes a sip of something fruity with an umbrella in it.

'Hung up your own coat for the night?' I hear myself say. Surprised at my own idiocy, I quickly tell him I'm sorry, again.

'I accept your apology,' he says with a wink and a nod, his floppy hair swaying like palm fronds. 'Let's dance for a bit.'

I can smell the grenadine and acerbic vodka on his mouth and see the thin sheen of sticky redness that clings to his lips like chapstick.

A sudden vision as he pulls me towards the dance floor, past the semi-naked bodies and through the turbid heat that hits so heavy it makes my arse crack leak sweat. I remember the flies that would buzz around the zapper in our backyard in summer, drawn by the sticky puddles of Coke and lemonade on the plastic outdoor table cover when my cousins and I would jostle for soft drinks. Then we would run to the trampoline, climbing up and jumping so hard and high that one of us would invariably vomit onto the concrete.

I succumb to the rhythm, awkwardly at first, with abrupt little steps, but then with more and more ease. Coat-check is swaying too, and when the beat drops, we jump up and down along with the whole crowd, like all of us have received a secret memo. Legs and arms akimbo, the napes of stout necks glistening and the pooling sweat at the bases of lower backs and beneath the folds of buttocks shining under the light. On and on with the technotronic beat, wooing us into ecstasy. The springs of the trampoline expanding, then shrinking taut again. Bodies colliding midair. Like when I was a kid, but this time Mum is not here to shout at me for going too near the edge.

This is pure exhibitionism: a trammelled longing bursting forth onto the stage in starlight and laser beams. I love the attention, the occasional glances from the muscle queens, but mostly the sweet eyes of Coat-check. His mouth forms into a smile as I dance goofily, legs and arms like the zigzags of a pharaoh.

'I just have to say, you are so hot,' I tell him.

'You are too!' he says.

I get a sudden vision of Saint Sebastian impaled by all those horny arrows. Our lips collide in a long kiss. The bitter gin taste in my mouth combines with his sweet fruitiness. I'm lost in his mouth and the feel of his neck in my palm, the grassy texture of his hair in my fingertips.

Then suddenly he pulls away, telling me he has to get back to the coat check. But I don't feel abandoned or sad, I just kiss him on the cheek and keep dancing. I do it for hours. Or is it days? Sometimes I'm joined by naked torsos, sometimes I'm by myself. The music takes me and it's 2am before I check my phone. Three missed calls from Dad. I look around; the floor has started emptying. I dance a bit more. I pee, missing the urinal and hitting the floor, holding my throbbing temple with my left hand.

After an Uber drive full of Afrobeat for an hour down the M5, I run up the stairs and fall onto my bed, still sticky, shining. I don't want to wash this euphoria off.

How to Have a Happy Marriage

The marriage bed is the beginning and end of pleasures.

My dad doesn't know his actual birthday. A clerical error in the village where he grew up means that he was born on either 3 May or 4 May. Whenever his birthday, 4 May is also my parents' wedding anniversary. This year will be their fortieth, so Rita and I have decided to make it a two-for-one deal and throw them a huge party.

Mum doesn't seem convinced that it should go ahead. 'I don't know why we have all this silliness about a party. Anyway, we will celebrate when you get married. Then we will throw the biggest party.'

Dad is silent on the subject, filling out a sudoku on the kitchen table with an air of deep concentration.

'Why don't you and Mum ever go on dates? Why aren't you romantic like the parents of my white friends?' I ask. My parents no longer sleep in the same room and barely speak.

'Fareed's idea of showing me a good time is taking me to the pharmacy,' Mum interjects, rolling out the dough for a batch of kahk.

'It's the only thing you have time for, always worrying and cleaning and whinge, whinge, whingeing like you have a gold medal in Olympic zen,' Dad responds. Zen is the Arabic expression for 'complaining'. Which is the exact opposite of the Buddhist notion of serenity.

Though my parents should have divorced long ago, I insist that their dysfunctional relationship and Dad's length of days are worth celebrating. But neither Rita nor I know how to cook, so we enlist some help and immediately call Tant Carmen. She is an expert on party catering on account of her early days working in a swanky hotel kitchen in Cairo.

'It's no problem for me to do this, habayeb,' Carmen begins. 'We just need to talk about who you want there, what the menu will be like, what the theme will be, the budget, where the kids will be seated, the list of allergies and dietary requirements, seating arrangements – you know, the basics.'

I go to my room to lie down: my head is swimming. I didn't know what I was getting myself into. The next morning I sit down with Rita and Tant Carmen at our kitchen table.

'Here is the guest list, which I wrote up last night.' She slips an extremely lengthy list across the table. I count two hundred names in total, many of them people I have never met.

Tant Carmen says there is nobody who can be cut from the

list without causing offence. She is even more adamant about the menu. 'I kept it simple because I know your parents are very modest people,' she says.

'J.Lo is not marrying Ben here, Carmen,' Rita objects. 'Tone it down with the theatrics.'

The list of menu items includes ten spatchcocked charcoal chickens from a shop called Ali Baba's Family Dinner, kousa ma7shi b el tamatem (stuffed zuchinni stewed with tomatoes), three dense round loaves of bread with the middles carved out and replaced with a tzatziki-style dip, twelve trays of macarona bechamel, molokheya and finally ma2louba, which means 'upside down' and gets its name from the way the chicken and rice are cooked in a pot and then flipped onto a serving platter. 'You make me ma2loub, woman, with your constant worrying!' is a dad joke that I hear my father say whenever Mum is making this last dish.

Carmen also insists that we will need bonbonnières: small parcels containing lollies and Bible verses so that 'people won't go home empty-handed with a bad taste in their mouth and give us the eye'.

On the morning of the party, Hossein, our elderly Persian family friend and butcher, arrives. My dad jokingly calls him 'the Butcher of Tabriz', and I have only ever seen him in a white, slightly bloodied rubber apron. He has always been a bit of a black sheep, periodically reciting the verses of the Sufi mystic Rumi without context. One thing he has done very well since we were small, however, is to source, skewer and spit-roast a whole lamb for every Easter get-together or Christmas lunch we have ever had.

Hossein carries the carcass to the bonfire area in the middle of the backyard, shoves the poor creature across the length of a full-metal skewer and sets it atop the barbecue pit. He speaks over it in the gentle words of the poet Kahlil Gibran: 'By the same power that slays you, I too am slain; and I too shall be consumed. For the law that delivered you into my hand shall deliver me into a mightier hand.' Then he slathers the lamb with a mixture of canola oil, oregano and garlic and sets it on fire.

I hand him an envelope of cash and go to usher in Milov, the party-hire man with wide-set eyes and broad cheeks that speak to his Slavic origins. He has parked his ute in the driveway, pylons, canvas tarpaulins and pyramid-style canvas roofs hanging out the back. I found him under a Bankstown-Canterbury area Facebook Marketplace listing that said, 'Same-day marquee set-up'.

Milov walks in gruffly, with the slightly hunched bearing and furrowed brow of Mikhail Gorbachev, and opens a thick binder onto the dining table, sitting heavily with an *oufft*.

'Dis particular marquee is called the "axis of power". It will destroy your grass but it looks very impressive. Dis particular marquee is ... Actually, we don't sell that one anymore, and dis one is called the "iron curtain" because it's heavy and thick. It'll stand for hours but it can fall suddenly, so we'll need to prop it up with some bricks,' he says, flicking through his binder.

I tell Milov I'd like the 'axis of power' and he gets to work immediately, bursting into action quicker than you would think his stout body could move – quicker even than Poland leaving the Soviet Union.

Though I told Mum that she needn't do anything today, it doesn't stop her from busying herself in the kitchen. She has been up since seven, baking, cooking and cleaning. Dad is also occupied with small and irrelevant tasks like resetting all the wristwatches in the house and oiling the door hinges with WD-40.

'When you are married, I will not only make maa3moul, I will cover the bride in tulle!' Mum laughs merrily at her little rhyme, then removes her rubber Croc to swat a fly that has landed on the stove.

It's two o'clock now, and Tant Carmen enters with Uncle Kareem, Shoukry and Ayman. Carmen is setting up trestle tables to bear the weight of all the food she has brought, which she lays out in aluminium trays. Shoukry and Ayman join Hossein with the lamb, and I overhear Carmen and Mum's conversation.

'As you know, we're not actually sure of Fareed's birthday,' Mum says. 'They kept such poor records in the village that it could either be May third or May fourth.'

Carmen nods knowingly.

'Mama told me that it would be better for me in Australia,' Mum continues, 'and that if I wanted any kind of a life, I should get on the boat and come here. Then she got sick, and she wanted me pregnant before she died. She died anyway, and then we had Rita.' Mum motions to my sister, who looks up abruptly from filing her nails at the mention of her name.

'Marriage is a curse, but children are a blessing,' Carmen says, and both she and Mum nod vigorously.

People have arrived and are getting hungry, so I go to Hossein to enquire about the lamb while Rita puts the desserts on tiny plates.

'Oh, yes, the little hills of Tehran were green and rolling like the clouds over the valley, which the famous Rumi described as—' he begins.

'Yes, yes, Hossein, that's fine, but when do you think the lamb will be ready?' I say, watching him slowly turning the spit.

'Soon, soon enough ...' he says, tearing off a large strip of burnished meat from its leg.

More people arrive: second cousins, family friends, a small flock of church ladies all dressed in black. Cousin Layla, ever the entrepreneur, tells Mum that she plans on selling Bessemer pots today – 'Just a few, really, you won't even notice.' Kids run around the lamb, stopping to tear off bits of meat for themselves, like something out of *Lord of the Flies*.

Dad has stationed himself in the hallway with his old mates from Telecom, where he worked throughout the 80s. They are all bawdy and rowdy in their very short shorts, thick white socks, sneakers and prominent beer bellies. They're already halfway in the bag.

'Your dad was a lucky bastard to have married a woman as beautiful as your mum,' one of them shouts at me.

'Fareed, do you remember that time we all crowded into your Ford, I think it was the Maverick model, and we drove down

Parramatta Road to see if we could pick up chicks, and the cops pulled us over and made us show our licences because they didn't like so many wogs being in one car?'

They all laugh, and Dad says, 'I miss that car.'

I walk into the family room to catch a breather and find that Layla has set up an elaborate display of heavy, red-lidded copper pots in a kind of pyramid structure. 'There's nothing better than Bessemer. The heavy copper base conducts heat, allowing the meat to steam while it roasts,' she says, slightly dead in the eyes. 'The large model is called the Colosseum and there's also an Acropolis package, which includes three heavy-based stovetop pots.'

'Jesus, Layla, it's a party, not a shopping centre,' Rita tells her. Nobody minds, though, and Mum has joined the women to carefully examine Layla's wares. 'Is there a returns policy?' she asks.

'Be careful, she will buy all the pots, use them and then exchange them for better models,' Tant Carmen jokes.

All the women cackle at Mum's thriftiness, and I head back to the backyard as Layla moves on to the topic of crockery. Hossein is still slowly turning the lamb on the spit, and I am disappointed to find that it has been almost completely stripped bare of meat.

'Like the songs of Tabriz ... fullness gives way to emptiness, but lo, the fullness cometh again,' he declares.

'Who put this fucking idiot in charge of the lamb?' Uncle Kareem asks.

It's now five o'clock. A disco ball is projecting colourful

lights onto the wall of Milov's huge but lopsided 'axis of power'. The smell of rendered lamb fat wafts sweetly through the air and all our cousins, young and old, are dancing to 'Shik Shak Shok', which is blaring through Shoukry's speakers. The girls are thrusting their hips out, up and down to the tune of the song.

Inside, people are sitting in the formal lounge, which has become a de facto marriage-arrangement office. There is a lot of silent flirting between the parties: those who have freshly arrived from Egypt and Australian-born cousins.

My cousin Nereen, who just got her permanent residency, is being asked to speak to an older 'freshie' relation, who is in his early forties and has come straight from Egypt. Though there is a ten-year age difference between them, we suspect there is another reason why Nereen seems so reluctant. Her mother says that she's a young princess waiting for the right man to sweep her off her feet, but her comfortable shoes say otherwise.

I hear Carmen clearing her throat over the microphone outside. We all head out to find her standing on a small platform, which Milov has expertly erected in the middle of the marquee. By propping it up like this, he said it would make a better 'perestroika against corruption', which seemed irrelevant to the topic of party hire.

With everyone having now eaten their fill, it's time for the formalities to get underway. 'Okay, everybody, please pay attention now. Rita, put the kobeba away, please,' Carmen shouts, generating a feedback screech.

'As you know, Samira and Fareed have been married for forty years.'

At this, there are claps from the crowd and some jeers from Dad's old work friends.

'Yes, yes, and it has been a beautiful marriage, full of happy moments … so many moments,' Carmen adds, 'so we will now have some words from their children.'

My parents have made many sacrifices to offer my sister and I the kind of life we enjoy. Mum missed her own mother's funeral because Dad couldn't take time off from the factory where he worked night shifts, and there was nobody else who could take care of us. 'You kids complain, complain, complain – never thinking to ask about your poor parents. Think of what we've been through,' Mum would often tell us in childhood.

So, it's with this in mind that Rita and I rise to the podium. I begin: 'There's so much we have to thank Mum and Dad for – protecting us, placing a roof over our heads and their years of devotion.'

My older aunties and uncles nod and smile at the very satisfactory gratitude and dutifulness.

Then Rita Chimes in: 'Most of all, I am grateful that they showed us what *not* to do to have a happy relationship. Hey, marriage is a construct anyway. Like virginity!'

All the millennials cheer, or at least those who aren't distracted by their phones. Uncle Kareem is dancing by himself in the corner and Nereen has stepped well clear from her older male suitor. Carmen awkwardly clears her throat and almost pushes me off the stage in her eagerness to move us along.

'Now Fareed's old school friend, Bob, will give a few words,' she says.

With a drunken slur and a lopsided gait from too many years of hitting the bottle, Bob, short for Nabil, rises to the podium. 'Bob has seen better days,' I hear Carmen tell Rita, who nods gravely.

'Fareed! Hardest at work! First to come, last to leave.' This generates many cheers from his colleagues. 'And Samira ...' At this, there is a palpable tension rising in Dad's face and something like longing in Bob's dark, vacant eyes. 'What a supermodel!'

Everyone is shaking their heads, embarrassed at how this has gone down. In our community, it's very bad form to comment on another man's wife so publicly.

'Okay, Bob, thank you, Bob,' Carmen says hurriedly, shooing him offstage. 'And now it's time for the man of the hour, Fareed, to give his speech.'

Dad takes the stage. With his hunched shoulders and little vest, he reminds me of Bilbo Baggins at his own birthday party.

'What beautiful faces! Don't know half of you, but here we are.' Dad clears his throat before continuing, and I hear Milov chewing loudly on a chicken skewer.

'People ask, why did I come to this country? Well, we had to do it! No choice! House was bombed by the Israelis. Then I met Samira, a beauty! We only had two witnesses, my sister and Samira's dad, and it was all worth it, not just to escape the war but to make a better life for all of you.'

Dad's morose contemplations elicit wet eyes, smiles and Arabic exclamations of 'Ya Rab! Oh Lord!' from across the audience.

'Now our kids are our pride,' Dad adds, beaming at us.

'Not married yet, though, are they?' Tant Carmen interjects.

Dad continues, ignoring his sister. 'Above all, I want to thank my lady. My number one. Samira, you have been a *godsend*.' He says this with a slight blubber and then walks off the stage, his cheeks shining with tears.

Mum nods like a magistrate, her stoic face hard as granite.

'Right, thank you, Fareed,' Carmen says. 'And happy birthday for today or tomorrow.'

It's time for the cutting of the giant Costco cake. It's enormous, encased in chocolate sprinkles and luminous with the sheen of a cocoa-butter frosting.

As the party ends, many people say they are leaving but linger in the hallway for at least half an hour. Some of them return for a quick second meal or some of Carmen's black oriental-style coffee, fragrant with cardamon and bitter in taste.

'It is bad if anyone leaves empty-handed,' Tant Carmen told me before the party got underway, so tonight everyone receives a party gift bag. In each bag, there are three slightly concave Lindt milk-chocolate balls, sugar-coated almonds and a tiny statue of the Christ Child of Prague covered in muslin cloth. Each bag also contains a card that says, 'Thank you for coming to Samira and Fareed's annivarsary.' The typo does not distract from the subtle beauty of the giant calligraphy.

When people finally leave, they hand over their own small gifts. I am given nine of the same Ferrero Rocher boxes, no doubt the result of an incestuous regift cycle from Christmas or Easter.

Rita and I slump down onto the couch in the family room, exhausted, and look at the bill. The cost of the equipment, the printing of the cards, the food – the whole thing is way in excess of what we expected because of Carmen's lengthy guest list and costs us all of our take-home pay.

Milov, who stayed all night to ensure 'a smooth transition of power', mistakenly asks Dad for his money. 'That'll be $500, please, for the cost of the marquee,' Milov grunts.

'Five hundred?' Dad responds. 'That's bloody highway robbery, Milov.' We usher our father down the corridor, assuring him we will bargain Milov down.

Rita and I split the cost across three credit cards, taking solace in the fact that we will inherit this house when our parents die.

Mum turns to us. 'See how beautiful a marriage can be?' she says. Dad tries to kiss her but she gently pushes his face away.

How to Buy a House

A man may leave no legacy, save for a semidetached granny flat.

I'm almost thirty-three, the 'Jesus age', and don't own any property yet. Dad keeps saying that it's now or never in terms of entering the market, on account of a global pandemic having slashed house prices.

Around the same time that our family's mortgage broker, Wanees Wanees, advised that was time to 'sell, sell, sell', Rita and I inherited about $80,000 from the sale of Gidoo's old bungalow with yellowing carpets. It was a whole thing getting the cash, with Tant Carmen and Uncle Kareem arguing with Dad over how the money should be split. In the end, Dad put his foot down and managed to get the money split four ways to double the share that we would receive as his children. 'My kids deserve a future!'

Now that I actually have dollars in the bank, I'm afraid

to part with them. Dad flies into a rage. 'The money is more valuable in property, you donkey!'

There are heaps of small units up on housesales.com, right near my work. They're clean, bright and just within my price range.

'This is very stupid,' Dad tells me. 'You may as well flush your money down the toilet if you intend on buying gyprock – the yield is very bad on your investment. Are you a donkey? I'm convinced you're a donkey.'

I keep looking, finding a neat two-room apartment in Ashwood with great natural light.

'It's on the bad side of the neighbourhood,' Dad tells me.

There's another with an intercom, a lift and a very spacious floor plan.

'You would be a 7omar to give them that asking price.'

I fall in love with a well-appointed unit with hardwood floors near Ashfield train station.

'Mould,' Dad says. 'Covered in mould.'

This goes on for two months before I decide it's time to call in the big guns and speak with our mortgage broker, who moonlights as a real estate agent and also an accountant. Though his hairline is receding and his floral shirt is stretched tight over his burgeoning belly, Wanees retains a kind of evergreen youthful vigour, like a flowering cactus in the desert. He also gives me lots of unsolicited advice about where to put my money.

'Now, I help a lot of people with preparing their loan applications, but I also give financial advice. It's very important that you buy well. I know you want to be comfortable and live conveniently ... but convenience cannot be the foundation for a successful future, mate,' Wanees begins.

He insists that I should purchase a large and spacious property in the suburbs, rent out for a year or two, sell it and then use the money to buy another, better property, also in the western suburbs. I should not venture to live in these houses, he says, but rent them out as soon as possible to trustworthy strangers, preferably wealthy Chinese exchange students because 'they pay top dollar'.

He goes on to say that there are lots of up-and-coming places in the far west where I should actually live. They offer an excellent yield and have verdant, promising names like Kimbalee Downs, Shoalhaven Way, Summerfield Plains and Greenhills. I blank out momentarily and return to consciousness to hear the end of Wanees' monologue.

'Obviously, it's your choice, mate, and you can do as you wish – congratulations on the loan.' Wanees has secured me an excellent conditional loan at a 3.31 per cent variable interest rate for a period of thirty years.

I go back into the market with renewed vigour. This time, I take Mum, who is as fretful and erratic as an angry cat, along with Rita to do a bit of property hunting.

'You need to listen to us ... learn from our mistakes,' they say. With her share of the money, Rita quickly bought a duplex to rent out while she continued living with our parents. It was condemned last week because the roof, we discovered, is full of asbestos.

I see heaps of properties over the next few months, but the Ashfield place is all I can think about. Nothing else feels right – like a husband cheating on his true love, I imagine. The mouldy apartment is right near the *Inner West Courier* and is within walking distance of bars and restaurants.

The real estate agent, an Italian guy in a polyester suit, eyes me with a squinty glare as I walk into the apartment block's driveway. 'There are many other expressions of interest so, honestly, mate, if you don't get in now, this thing will be eaten up in hours,' he says immediately, despite the fact that it has been available for months.

I tell Dad, who is standing with his arms folded on the kerbside, that I'm not interested. But when his back is turned, I give the agent my number and tell him to send me the contract immediately. At home, I start having misgivings. I wonder if I've gone into this thing too quickly, so I draw up a list of pros and cons.

Pros:

- Close to city
- Far from western suburbs
- Nice new floorboards and good view

Cons:

- Too many hipsters
- Shit food and incompetent white barbers
- Live next door to a pub, drunks, probably meth heads

My mind isn't made up, so I walk into my parents' room with my ears ringing and my heart in my throat. I know I must get this out. I have to test the waters. Mum is eating salted pistachios from the shell and Dad is playing Candy Crush on his giant Huawei P30 Pro.

'Mum, Dad, I'm buying that apartment,' I say.

Mum's bowl of nuts cascades off her leg and onto the floor as she stands abruptly, eyes ablaze and nose flaring. 'If you buy this terrible small unit in the inner city, you will bring me down to the grave with shame,' she says. 'Do you think such a place is acceptable for a wife? What girl will be pleased with this kind of a hovel?' she adds in Arabic.

'Well, I like it, and that's more important than any wife,' I tell her. Dad shakes his head.

Mum says, 'Rabena yeshfee.' May God heal.

I call Wanees for advice but I get his voicemail: 'With Wanees Wanees home financing, the property chooses *you*,' it says in the booming voice of a paid commercial actor.

I set the phone down, exhaling slowly. The apartment listing is open on my laptop, the photos bright and inviting. It looks right. It feels right. But does that mean it's right?

My parents don't think so. 'Too soon.' 'Too rushed.' 'You can find better.' Their words echo in my head, mixing with my own doubts. For them, an apartment isn't just a place to live, it's the springboard for a *proper* life, with enough room for little feet to run around. Am I just being stubborn? Trying to prove something? I want to be sure, to know that my desperation to escape my parents isn't clouding my judgement.

I run through the pros and cons again, as if a perfect balance will suddenly reveal itself. It's in a good location, right in the heart of the Inner West, which hipsters colonised after my parents escaped it in the 80s. The layout makes sense. The price is ... manageable. The mould, removable. But the unease sits heavy in my chest. I'm not just buying an apartment – I am choosing a life. But, sooner or later, I have to make this decision myself.

On a podcast called *Bliss Hacks*, I once heard a white lady called Tiffany St Clare say that sleeping on a tricky choice can offer clarity. That night, dropping into a fitful state of limbo, I feel a heavy burden on my chest. I am laid out on the floor in the good room. A heavy piece of furniture sits on my stomach, ornate chair legs bruising my ribs, the full weight of a chaise lounge bearing down on me. Then my dad, with a cup of tea in hand, walks over and sits on it. As he slurps merrily, unphased by my screams, Mum runs over with a plate of food and force-feeds mokorona into my gaping mouth. I choke on pasta. My sternum cracks under the pressure.

I wake screaming. I'm sticky with sweat. I breathe deeper to try to calm myself. Cursing Tiffany's suggestion and wondering whether she is even an accredited psychologist, I shower and watch an episode of *El Hajj Metwalee's Wives* on my laptop. I do make a decision, though, and for better or worse, I stick with it.

That morning, I call the real estate agent. 'I'll take it. Send me the contract!' I shout, hanging up before he can answer. I feel lighter, freer. I feel new.

That's until I visit the apartment again that afternoon and realise how much there is to do. This will not be easy. I make some calls to Jawad and Abanoub, telling them I need some contractors. They give me the hook-up through some church friends, and the head tradie at a construction firm called Maroun Developments shows me his plans that weekend. Distracted by the girthy leg muscles sticking out of his khaki work shorts, I will myself to focus. We settle on some tile choices, some new spotlights to brighten the place and a bathroom plan. When it comes time to talk cost, I agree to his first price, too exhausted and relieved to barter.

Over the next two months, I watch the apartment transform: the mould in the ceiling is covered with an antifungal kind of paint; the hardwood is polished and buffed; the kitchen cabinets, once shitty laminate, are now a shinier faux-granite fibro.

This place has nothing on my family home, a sprawling double-storey in the suburbs, replete with plush Persian carpets, chandelier-style lighting bedecked with hundreds of tiny plastic crystals, bathrooms with built-in bidets in each toilet and a pergola-covered outdoor area for family barbecues. Whenever aunts and uncles visit from Egypt, they announce, 'Kbeer 2wi ya Fareed. Zo2ik momtaz ya Samira.' It's so spacious, Fareed. You have beautiful taste, Samira. Despite Rita constantly hogging the TV or yelling at me to get out of the bathroom because I am taking too long, this house has made me feel like Richie Rich.

My stomach problems pretty much disappeared after I finished uni, came out, got a job – but they still creep back whenever I have to tell my parents something important. So, it's with a knot in my stomach and a nervous tingling in my feet that I walk Mum and Dad through the new apartment three months later, hoping that it holds up to scrutiny. They take in the rooms, the shiny floors, the small balcony with its rows of potted plants, the whiteness of the walls, the neat cabinets of the kitchen and bathroom and the ample built-in wardrobes in the bedroom, with its bare and lonely double bed that I had delivered from Ikea.

'Not bad,' Dad concedes as he surveys the empty space.

Mum, ever practical, sets to work immediately – laying down fresh bed covers, mopping the floor and watering the plants. She wipes her hands on her oversized Mickey Mouse shirt, then straightens. 'You can live with us until you need to move here with your wife,' she says briskly, already making plans.

I don't respond.

As we drive home, the city unspools around us – the local shopping centre with its bustling Chinese grocers and Vietnamese bakeries gives way to rows of brick houses, then the great, unrelenting stretch of the M5. The car hums softly, the silence thick with unspoken things. I watch Dad's hands grip the wheel, his knuckles pale against the leather. Mum stares straight ahead. No one says a word. Mum's statement still hasn't been met with an answer. She doesn't seek one. Maybe she knows that I will never move in with a wife.

The road swallows us whole.

A Closing Thought: How to Have It All

The dog that bites is the dog that bites.

I've lived in my Ashfield apartment for six months now. I love my new place. The hardwood floors are clean and shiny, the synthetic white granite countertops resplendent under the kitchen downlights: particles of stone glittering like starlight.

To deck out the apartment, I went to Kmart for little things like my coffee table and kitchen supplies, and to Ikea for the fancy stuff: a yellow rug and a white canvas with a painting of a leaf. There are also the relics of Egyptian culture I have inherited from Mum: a painting of the bust of Tutankhamun and a picture of the Holy Family crossing the Nile Delta on a donkey.

As I settle in, a sense of ease and comfort washes over me. After working a few hours, interviewing local politicians about how they'll fix up the GreenWay or clean up the CBD, I'll go for a walk and grab some bread from the Vietnamese bakery and vegetables from the Chinese grocer. I cook, I clean, I have a wank and repeat it all. On Fridays and the weekend, I'll scroll Fumble, or Scruff if the mood should take me, sometimes going on a coffee date, sometimes inviting the bloke up if he catches my eye and the conversation is right. Most of the time, though, I eat Mum's leftover bamya and watch El Hajj Metwalee's wives hatch some outrageous scheme to get him to lose weight.

But at night, I hear bottles smashing at the pub next door and junkies screaming, 'Bitch dog cunt! You're a cunt! Rabies-infested cunt!' It's usually too late when the police come because the mob has already dispersed, like my hopes of sleep.

Deciding I need some company in the apartment, I google puppies on Yagoona pound's website. They are all terriers or mastiffs with the soulful, desperate eyes of prison inmates. Cute, but sad. But then, there is a boxer called Rex.

I first see him at the pound a week after googling the puppies. He is a huge seven-year-old, tawny save for his white chest and paws, and I feel immediate and visceral fear. My skin goes cold and my face hot. He looks so aggressive – nothing like the harmless childhood fantasies of Lassie types, slender and golden with bushy tails and playful demeanours. This is a man's dog, muscular and ugly. After signing the forms, I walk him to the car and he sits dolefully in the back, looking over his shoulder at the place he is leaving behind.

Rex is sceptical of me at first, eyeing me down with the critical look of a magistrate, which matches his jowly face. I soon realise that he walks with a limp. The website didn't mention that he was disabled.

Growing up, I treated our dogs as pets. Aladdin, Sultan and Pasha were good boys, but they all came to ignominious ends, from a stroke, a Toyota Corolla and a tick bite respectively. I fed them, occasionally walked them, but never got too attached. Above all else, they remained outside dogs.

I try to set the same boundaries with Rex. I buy him a bed from Petco, place it next to the balcony door and tell him to sit there. He does so for a while. His eyes are brown and huge, and they stare right back at you, unafraid. I wonder if he's thinking about his previous owner. What must he make of me and my tiny apartment? At that point he shambles in and licks my face.

Over the next few weeks, he explores the rest of the apartment, first to the carpet in front of the TV, then sitting outside the bathroom while waiting for me to finish showering, then to the foot of my bed. I wake up a few days later with him on top of me, his warmth radiating into me. I don't remember him climbing up in the night.

When Mum and Rita visit, they tell me off. Mum says Father Constantinos won't be able to bless a house with a dog in it. Rita says that we aren't white people, it's disgusting – where does he make kaka? But when I go on a walk with Rita to poop Rex and get some charcoal chicken, she's impressed with the way that people make space for him.

'Haven't you seen a boxer before, you little shits?' she shouts at a group of schoolkids who stare too long at his hobbled gait.

Mum visits again with Dad – she to make some kahk and to mop my kitchen, and he to watch Arsenal beat Man City. I walk into the kitchen to find Mum patting Rex on the head and calling him habibi. Dad lets him sit on the couch and rubs his belly.

'See how the bloody players are all faffy boy show-offs, ya Rex!' Dad shouts at the sluggish dog, who raises his head in response.

After a long day at the *Inner West Courier*, writing inane stories about a local teen's Olympic rowing dreams or the musical line-up at the next Italian street fair, Rita comes over and we watch more of *El Hajj Metwalee's Wives*. We chew pumpkin seeds, spitting out the shells into pyramid mounds on the coffee table.

One night I look through the kitchen window to see the junkie from the pub next door shitting into a bush. I'm grateful that Rex is toilet-trained, and I shut the blinds. I walk across the cold tiles and into the bathroom to do my night skincare routine: I use a Korean salicylic facewash and apply my CeraVe moisturising cream. Then I say the Jesus Prayer: 'Jesus Christ, Son of God, have mercy on me, a sinner.' I open my bible, read Ecclesiastes 4, which says, 'Two are better than one. If either of them falls down, one can help the other up. If two lie down together, they will keep warm.'

At two in the morning, I awake to the sound of Rex's moaning. Sometimes he has nightmares like this, the fur on his brow creasing and his giant barrel chest rapidly moving up and down. I gently stroke his tummy and neck, nudging him awake. He blinks up at me, his gentle warm breath on my arm, his eyes sweet and full of trust. Then he growls, first low and guttural, and then in sharp, high yelps.

I turn the light on, my heart beating hard in my neck. His mouth is dribbling with more saliva than usual; no, scratch that, he is frothing at the mouth. Rex rises to a standing position and his hackles are up. He bares his teeth at me, less sweetly than before. Then he pounces at me and I duck, knocking over my Ikea Årstid dimmer lamp in my haste. The glass cracks on the floor and some of it pierces the soft flesh of my foot in jagged shards. I run to the kitchen, Rex lunging after me, and grab a rolling pin.

'Rexxy, no!' I shout as he weaves around me, pouncing again.

I make for the living room, but he bites me hard through the fabric of my new Kmart 'sleepy comforts' range pyjama pants. A dull, beating pain begins to spread where his teeth have met flesh. I pin him down and knock him over the head hard with the rolling pin. His face goes slack and I wrap him in my new Kmart plush-feel living room blanket, my knee on his chest.

Later at the vet, they say that Rex contracted rabies. I don't remember him licking a dead cat or rat, but either way, he has to be put down. I have to pay $500 and sign a waiver that says that Ashfield Pets R Family is not responsible for Rex's death. My leg is wrapped in gauze and a tetanus needle is injected hard into the bony part of my shoulder.

Dad shakes his head in the driver's seat, after coming all the way from the west at four in the morning to be here with me. He sucks his teeth while I cry in the passenger seat.

'See, this is why you don't let dogs in the house.'

How to Pay Your Dues

Deep thanks all round, but above all:

To my partner, Kashif Harrison, whose love has buoyed and steadied me these past two years and with whom I have built a home and a life. His patience, his habit of telling me to 'stop squinting' in photos and his dedication to capturing and sharing my work have made me feel treasured and lucky. He has also fathered our kids, Otto and Lyla – who, biologically, are dogs.

To Michael Mohammed Ahmad and Winnie Dunn. Mohammed, my great mentor and friend, put me forward for the Affirm Press Mentorship for Sweatshop Writers, which resulted in the book you hold in your hands. The concern and kindness he gives the writers he works with, not just to their work but for their wellbeing, has rightly made him the champion of a new wave of Australian literature. Winnie is my sister, lending an open heart and ear as I navigate the struggle to find my voice. Thanks also to the wider Sweatshop community for their sharp editorial insight – you are the finest peers and collaborators.

To Martin Hughes, Ruby Ashby-Orr and the entire Affirm Press team for their faith in me, their empathy and skill. And to Camha Pham and Zoe Sorenson, whose thoughtful edits significantly improved this book, and to Armelle Davies for her proofread.

I am grateful to my family, especially my parents, whose courage and sacrifice gave me the privilege of choice and the freedom to make art, as well as my sisters, for their relentless love. It hasn't always been easy, but they've always been there.

Family too in Adam Novaldy Anderson, Adrian Mouhajer, Annalise Awkar, Aylin Ciden, Cindy Nour, Ece Egilmezer, Elise Marcus, Glenn Noble, Liam Smith, Luisa Albiero, Mark Mariano, Natalia Figueroa Barroso, Patrice Moriarty, Sally Hurley, Sarah Ayoub, Sheree Joseph, Shirley Le, Sophia Nasser and Vivienne Lam – in moments of uncertainty, they have held me down, lifted me up and reminded me of the bigger picture.

Finally, to Radhika and Adrian Sukumar-White and the entire Leichhardt Uniting Church community – a safe harbour in the storm where grace knows no exclusions.